Better Homes and Gardens®

COOKIES COOKIES COOKIES
Any-Day Treats

BETTER HOMES AND GARDENS® BOOKS
Des Moines

COOKIES, COOKIES, COOKIES
Editor: Shelli McConnell
Graphic Designer: Tom Wegner
Associate Department Editor: Elizabeth Woolever
Associate Art Director: Linda Ford Vermie
Publishing Systems Text Processor: Paula Forest
Cover Food Stylists: Lynn Blanchard, Janet Herwig
Cover Photographer: Mike Dieter

BETTER HOMES AND GARDENS® BOOKS
An Imprint of Meredith® Books
President, Book Group: Joseph J. Ward
Vice President and Editorial Director: Elizabeth P. Rice
Executive Editor: Connie Schrader
Food and Family Life Editor: Sharyl Heiken
Art Director: Ernest Shelton
Managing Editor: David A. Kirchner
Prepress Production Manager: Randall Yontz
Test Kitchen Director: Sharon Stilwell

WE CARE!

All of us at Better Homes and Gardens® Books are dedicated to providing you with the information and ideas you need to create tasty foods. We welcome your comments or suggestions. Write us at: Better Homes and Gardens® Books, Cookbook Editorial Department, 1716 Locust Street, Des Moines, IA 50309-3023

If you would like to order additional copies of any of our books, call 1-800-678-2803 or check with your local bookstore.

Our seal assures you that every recipe in *Cookies, Cookies, Cookies* has been tested in the Better Homes and Gardens® Test Kitchen. This means that each recipe is practical and reliable, and meets our high standards of taste appeal. We guarantee your satisfaction with this book for as long as you own it.

Any-Day Treats

Any time of the year, any day of the week, or any minute of the hour is the time for fresh, full-of-flavor cookies. When they're piping hot from the oven or dunked deep into milk, nothing beats 'em.

Cookie Recipes in this Book

Pictured on the cover: Almond Biscotti, Cherry-Pecan Rounds, Choco-Candy Cookies, Chocolate-Peanut Butter Bars, Eggnog Kringla, Peanut Butter-Oatmeal Rounds, Slice-of-Orange Cookies, Greek Honey-Walnut Balls, Lemon-Almond Tea Cookies, Snickerdoodles, Sugar Cookie Cutouts, Swedish Butter Cookies (see recipe listing above for page numbers).

All-Occasion Cookie Favorites

Create new memories for youngsters and renew old ones for grown-ups with toothsome treats from the cookie jar. Fill it with old-fashioned classics such as Snickerdoodles and Chocolate Crinkles or with new-found favorites such as Oatmeal-Caramel Bars and Almond Meringues.

Snickerdoodles (see recipe, page 44)

Peanut Butter-Oatmeal Rounds
(see recipe, page 15)

For a gourmet cookie, try the macadamia version with 1 cup chopped white baking bars (or pieces) and 1 cup semisweet chocolate pieces.

Chocolate Chip Cookies

½   **cup shortening**
½   **cup margarine *or* butter**
2½ **cups all-purpose flour**
 1 **cup packed brown sugar**
½   **cup sugar**
 2 **eggs**
 1 **teaspoon vanilla**
½   **teaspoon baking soda**
 1 **12-ounce package (2 cups) semisweet chocolate pieces**
 1 **cup chopped walnuts, pecans, *or* hazelnuts (filberts) (optional)**

🌰 In a large mixing bowl beat the shortening and margarine or butter with an electric mixer on medium to high speed about 30 seconds or till softened. Add about *half* of the flour to the shortening mixture. Then add brown sugar, sugar, eggs, vanilla, and baking soda. Beat till thoroughly combined, scraping sides of bowl occasionally. Beat in remaining flour. Stir in the chocolate pieces and walnuts, pecans, or hazelnuts.

🌰 Drop the dough by rounded teaspoons 2 inches apart onto ungreased cookie sheets. Bake in a 375° oven for 8 to 10 minutes or till edges are lightly browned. Remove cookies and cool on wire racks. Makes about 60.

Nutrition information per cookie: 87 calories, 1 g protein, 13 g carbohydrate, 4 g fat (1 g saturated), 7 mg cholesterol, 28 mg sodium, 38 mg potassium.

Macadamia Nut and White Chocolate Chunk Cookies: Prepare Chocolate Chip Cookies as directed at left, *except* substitute chopped *white baking bars (or pieces) or vanilla-flavored candy coating* for the semisweet chocolate pieces and substitute one 3½-ounce jar *macadamia nuts,* chopped, for the nuts.

Nutrition information per cookie: 103 calories, 1 g protein, 13 g carbohydrate, 6 g fat (2 g saturated), 7 mg cholesterol, 33 mg sodium, 43 mg potassium.

Frosted Pumpkin Drops

½ **cup shortening**
½ **cup margarine *or* butter**
2 **cups all-purpose flour**
1 **cup sugar**
1 **cup canned pumpkin**
2 **eggs**
1½ **teaspoons pumpkin pie spice**
1 **teaspoon baking soda**
¼ **teaspoon salt**
1 **cup raisins**
1 **3-ounce package cream cheese**
¼ **cup margarine *or* butter**
1 **teaspoon vanilla**
2 **cups sifted powdered sugar**

In a large mixing bowl beat the shortening and ½ cup margarine or butter with an electric mixer on medium to high speed about 30 seconds or till softened. Add about *half* of the flour to the shortening mixture. Then add the sugar, pumpkin, eggs, pumpkin pie spice, baking soda, and salt. Beat mixture till thoroughly combined, scraping the sides of bowl occasionally. Beat in the remaining flour. Stir in the raisins.

Drop the dough by rounded tablespoons 2 inches apart onto ungreased cookie sheets. Bake in a 375° oven for 10 to 12 minutes or till edges are lightly browned. Remove cookies and cool on wire racks.

Meanwhile, for frosting, in a small mixing bowl beat the cream cheese, ¼ cup margarine or butter, and vanilla till well combined. Gradually add the powdered sugar and beat till smooth. Spread frosting over cooled cookies. Makes about 28.

Nutrition information per cookie: 194 calories, 2 g protein, 25 g carbohydrate, 10 g fat (3 g saturated), 19 mg cholesterol, 120 mg sodium, 77 mg potassium.

An orange-flavored cookie that's chock-full of chewy dates and mild, sweet hazelnuts.

Hazelnut-Date Cookies

  2 **cups all-purpose flour**
  1 **teaspoon baking powder**
      Dash salt
  ½ **cup margarine** *or* **butter**
  1 **cup sugar**
  1 **egg**
  1 **teaspoon finely shredded orange** *or*
      lemon peel
  1 **teaspoon vanilla**
  ⅓ **cup orange juice**
1½ **cups ground hazelnuts (filberts)**
      (6 ounces)
1¼ **cups snipped pitted dates**
      Blanched whole hazelnuts (filberts),
      toasted (optional)

🍂 In a medium mixing bowl combine the flour, baking powder, and salt. Set aside.

🍂 In a large mixing bowl beat margarine or butter with an electric mixer on medium to high speed about 30 seconds or till softened. Add sugar and beat till fluffy. Add egg, orange or lemon peel, and vanilla. Beat well, scraping the sides of the bowl occasionally. Stir in the orange juice, then the flour mixture. Stir in the ground nuts and snipped dates.

🍂 Drop dough by rounded teaspoons 2 inches apart onto greased cookie sheets. If desired, top each mound with a whole nut. Bake in a 350° oven for 10 to 12 minutes or till edges are lightly browned. Remove cookies and cool on wire racks. Makes about 48.

Nutrition information per cookie: 87 calories, 1 g protein, 12 g carbohydrate, 4 g fat (1 g saturated), 10 mg cholesterol, 30 mg sodium, 56 mg potassium.

8

Rich, luscious cream cheese frosting enhances these delightfully tangy cookies.

Lemon Drops

½ cup shortening
½ cup margarine *or* butter
 2 cups all-purpose flour
¾ cup sugar
⅓ cup milk
 1 tablespoon finely shredded lemon peel
    Lemon-Cream Cheese Frosting
    Candied lemon peel (optional)

🐢 In a large mixing bowl beat shortening and margarine or butter with an electric mixer on medium to high speed about 30 seconds or till softened. Add about *half* of the flour to the shortening mixture. Then add the sugar, milk, and finely shredded lemon peel. Beat till thoroughly combined, scraping the sides of bowl occasionally. Then beat or stir in the remaining flour.

🐢 Drop dough by rounded teaspoons 2 inches apart onto ungreased cookie sheets. Bake in a 375° oven about 10 minutes or till edges are lightly browned. Remove cookies and cool on wire racks. Frost with Lemon Cream-Cheese Frosting. If desired, garnish with candied lemon peel. Store, covered, in the refrigerator. Makes about 48.

Lemon-Cream Cheese Frosting: In a medium mixing bowl beat ½ of an 8-ounce package *cream cheese* and ¼ cup softened *margarine or butter* till well combined. Beat in 1 cup sifted *powdered sugar* and 2 tablespoons *lemon juice* till smooth. Beat in 2¼ to 2½ cups additional sifted *powdered sugar* till frosting is of spreading consistency.

Nutrition information per cookie: 97 calories, 1 g protein, 11 g carbohydrate, 6 g fat (2 g saturated), 3 mg cholesterol, 41 mg sodium, 13 mg potassium.

A soft spiced cookie, with raisins or without.

Oatmeal-Carrot Cookies

¾ cup margarine *or* butter
1¾ cups all-purpose flour
¾ cup packed brown sugar
½ cup sugar
1 egg
1 teaspoon baking powder
1 teaspoon vanilla
½ teaspoon ground cinnamon
¼ teaspoon baking soda
¼ teaspoon ground cloves
2 cups rolled oats
1 cup finely shredded carrots
½ cup raisins (optional)

🐢 In a large mixing bowl beat the margarine or butter with an electric mixer on medium to high speed about 30 seconds or till softened.

🐢 Add about *half* of the flour to the margarine. Then add the brown sugar, sugar, egg, baking powder, vanilla, cinnamon, baking soda, and cloves. Beat till thoroughly combined, scraping sides of bowl occasionally. Then beat or stir in the remaining flour. Stir in the rolled oats, finely shredded carrots, and, if desired, raisins.

🐢 Drop dough by rounded teaspoons 2 inches apart onto ungreased cookie sheets. Bake in a 375° oven for 10 to 12 minutes or till edges are lightly browned. Remove cookies and cool on wire racks. Makes about 48.

Nutrition information per cookie: 77 calories, 1 g protein, 11 g carbohydrate, 3 g fat (1 g saturated), 4 mg cholesterol, 51 mg sodium, 39 mg potassium.

Browned Butter Cookies

2½ cups all-purpose flour
  1 teaspoon baking soda
  ½ teaspoon baking powder
  ¼ teaspoon salt
1½ cups packed brown sugar
  ½ cup margarine *or* butter
  2 eggs
  1 teaspoon vanilla
  1 cup dairy sour cream
  1 cup coarsely chopped walnuts
     Browned Butter Icing

🌰 In a medium mixing bowl stir together the flour, baking soda, baking powder, and salt. Set aside.

🌰 In a large mixing bowl combine the brown sugar and margarine or butter. Beat with an electric mixer on medium speed till well combined. Beat in eggs and vanilla till fluffy. Add the flour mixture to margarine mixture along with the sour cream, mixing well. Stir in chopped nuts.

🌰 Drop by rounded teaspoons 2 inches apart onto greased cookie sheets. Bake in a 350° oven about 10 minutes or till set. Remove cookies and cool on wire racks. Frost with Browned Butter Icing. Makes about 56.

Browned Butter Icing: In a small saucepan heat ¼ cup *butter* (not margarine) over medium-low heat for 10 to 12 minutes or till lightly browned. Remove from heat. Stir in 2 cups sifted *powdered sugar* and enough *boiling water* (1 to 2 tablespoons) to make icing of spreading consistency. Frost cookies immediately. If frosting becomes grainy, soften with a few drops of hot water.

Nutrition information per cookie: 102 calories, 1 g protein, 14 g carbohydrate, 5 g fat (1 g saturated), 12 mg cholesterol, 61 mg sodium, 47 mg potassium.

A chocolaty delight even
without the lacy drizzle of
candy coating.

*S*weet Chocolate Cookies

½   **cup margarine** *or* **butter**
1¾ **cups all-purpose flour**
1   **cup sugar**
1   **4-ounce package sweet baking**
    chocolate, melted and cooled
2   **eggs**
¾   **teaspoon baking soda**
¼   **teaspoon salt**
½   **cup chopped nuts**
2   **ounces vanilla-flavored candy coating**
1   **teaspoon shortening**

In a large mixing bowl beat margarine or
butter with an electric mixer on medium to
high speed about 30 seconds or till softened.
Add about *half* of the flour to the margarine.
Then add the sugar, melted chocolate, eggs,
baking soda, and salt. Beat till thoroughly
combined, scraping the sides of bowl
occasionally. Then beat or stir in the remaining
flour. Stir in chopped nuts.

Drop dough by rounded teaspoons 2
inches apart onto ungreased cookie sheets.
Bake in a 375° oven for 10 to 12 minutes or
till cookies are set. Remove the cookies and
cool completely on wire racks.

In a small heavy saucepan melt candy
coating and shortening over low heat, stirring
occasionally. Drizzle over tops of cookies.
Makes about 48.

Nutrition information per cookie: 77 calories,
1 g protein, 10 g carbohydrate, 4 g fat (1 g saturated),
9 mg cholesterol, 50 mg sodium, 29 mg potassium.

Hermits

¾ cup margarine *or* butter
1½ cups all-purpose flour
¾ cup packed brown sugar
 1 egg
¼ cup strong brewed coffee, cooled
 1 teaspoon ground cinnamon
½ teaspoon baking soda
¼ teaspoon ground cloves
¼ teaspoon ground nutmeg
 2 cups raisins
 1 cup chopped pecans
    Pecan halves (optional)
    Sifted powdered sugar

☙ In a large mixing bowl beat margarine or butter with an electric mixer on medium to high speed about 30 seconds or till softened. Add about *half* of the flour to the margarine. Then add the brown sugar, egg, coffee, cinnamon, baking soda, cloves, and nutmeg. Beat till thoroughly combined, scraping the sides of bowl occasionally. Then beat or stir in the remaining flour. Stir in the raisins and chopped pecans.

☙ Drop dough by rounded tablespoons 2 inches apart onto ungreased cookie sheets. If desired, lightly press a pecan half on top of each mound.

☙ Bake in a 375° oven for 8 to 10 minutes or till edges are lightly browned. Remove cookies and cool on wire racks. Sprinkle with powdered sugar. Makes about 48.

Nutrition information per cookie: 88 calories, 1 g protein, 12 g carbohydrate, 5 g fat (1 g saturated), 4 mg cholesterol, 45 mg sodium, 74 mg potassium.

A crunchy pecan half and a dusting of powdered sugar garnish each tender cookie.

Soft, old-fashioned cookies with a delightful maple flavor.

Maple-Nut Drops

½ **cup margarine** *or* **butter**
1¼ **cups all-purpose flour**
⅓ **cup packed brown sugar**
¼ **cup maple syrup** *or* **maple-flavored syrup**
1 **egg**
1 **tablespoon milk**
½ **teaspoon baking soda**
¾ **cup chopped walnuts** *or* **pecans**
  Maple Frosting
¼ **cup finely chopped walnuts** *or* **pecans (optional)**

🌰 In a mixing bowl beat margarine or butter with an electric mixer on medium to high speed about 30 seconds or till softened.

🌰 Add about *half* of the flour to the margarine. Then add the brown sugar, maple or maple-flavored syrup, egg, milk, and baking soda. Beat till thoroughly combined, scraping sides of bowl occasionally. Beat or stir in the remaining flour. Stir in the ¾ cup chopped walnuts or pecans.

🌰 Drop dough by rounded teaspoons 2 inches apart onto ungreased cookie sheets. Bake in a 350° oven for 8 to 9 minutes or till edges are firm. Remove cookies and cool on wire racks. Frost cookies with Maple Frosting. If desired, sprinkle with ¼ cup finely chopped walnuts or pecans. Makes about 36.

Maple Frosting: In a small mixing bowl beat 2 tablespoons *maple syrup or maple-flavored syrup* and 2 tablespoons softened *margarine or butter* till well combined. Gradually beat in 1 to 1¼ cups sifted *powdered sugar* till frosting is of spreading consistency.

Nutrition information per cookie: 88 calories, 1 g protein, 11 g carbohydrate, 5 g fat (1 g saturated), 6 mg cholesterol, 55 mg sodium, 29 mg potassium.

Peanut butter and peanuts give these cookies an extra-nutty flavor.

Pictured on the cover and on page 5.

*P*eanut Butter-Oatmeal Rounds

¾ **cup margarine** *or* **butter**
½ **cup peanut butter**
1¼ **cups all-purpose flour**
1 **cup sugar**
½ **cup packed brown sugar**
2 **eggs**
1 **teaspoon baking powder**
1 **teaspoon vanilla**
½ **teaspoon baking soda**
2 **cups rolled oats**
1 **cup chopped cocktail peanuts** *or*
    semisweet chocolate pieces

🐦 In a large mixing bowl beat margarine or butter and peanut butter with an electric mixer on medium speed about 30 seconds or till combined.

🐦 Add about *half* of the flour to the margarine mixture. Then add the sugar, brown sugar, eggs, baking powder, vanilla, and baking soda. Beat till thoroughly combined, scraping the sides of bowl occasionally. Then beat or stir in the remaining flour. Stir in rolled oats and chopped peanuts or chocolate pieces.

🐦 Drop dough by rounded teaspoons 2 inches apart onto ungreased cookie sheets. Bake in a 375° oven about 10 minutes or till edges are lightly browned. Remove cookies and cool on wire racks. Makes about 60.

Nutrition information per cookie: 87 calories, 2 g protein, 10 g carbohydrate, 5 g fat (1 g saturated), 7 mg cholesterol, 51 mg sodium, 53 mg potassium.

15

Choose firm, tart baking apples for these flavorful cookies.

Spiced Apple Drops

½ **cup margarine** *or* **butter**
2 **cups all-purpose flour**
⅔ **cup sugar**
⅔ **cup packed brown sugar**
1 **egg**
¼ **cup apple juice** *or* **apple cider**
1 **teaspoon ground cinnamon**
½ **teaspoon baking soda**
½ **teaspoon ground nutmeg**
⅛ **teaspoon ground cloves**
1 **cup finely chopped apple**
1 **cup chopped walnuts**
   Apple Frosting

🍂 In a large mixing bowl beat margarine or butter with an electric mixer on medium to high speed about 30 seconds or till softened.
🍂 Add about *half* of the flour to the margarine. Then add the sugar, brown sugar, egg, *half* of the apple juice or cider, cinnamon, baking soda, nutmeg, and cloves. Beat till thoroughly combined, scraping sides of bowl occasionally. Then beat or stir in remaining flour and remaining apple juice or cider. Stir in chopped apple and walnuts.

🍂 Drop dough by rounded teaspoons 2 inches apart onto lightly greased cookie sheets. Bake in a 375° oven for 10 to 12 minutes or till edges are lightly browned. Cool on cookie sheets for 1 minute. Remove cookies and cool on wire racks. Frost with Apple Frosting. Store, covered, in the refrigerator. Makes about 40.

Apple Frosting: In a medium mixing bowl combine 4 cups sifted *powdered sugar,* ¼ cup softened *margarine or butter,* and 1 teaspoon *vanilla.* Beat in enough *apple juice or apple cider* (3 to 4 tablespoons) to make frosting of spreading consistency.

Nutrition information per cookie: 126 calories, 1 g protein, 19 g carbohydrate, 5 g fat (1 g saturated), 5 mg cholesterol, 52 mg sodium, 30 mg potassium.

If you have oat bran hot cereal on hand, substitute 1½ cups of it for the rolled oats. Then you won't need to turn oats into oat flour.

Oatmeal-Raisin 'n' Walnut Cookies

2 cups rolled oats
¾ cup margarine *or* butter
1 cup all-purpose flour
¾ cup sugar
¾ cup packed brown sugar
2 eggs
2 teaspoons finely shredded orange peel (optional)
1 teaspoon baking soda
1 teaspoon vanilla
½ teaspoon ground cinnamon
¼ teaspoon ground nutmeg
1½ cups raisins *or* one 8-ounce package chopped pitted dates
1 cup chopped walnuts

🍂 For oat flour, in a blender container place ½ *cup* of the rolled oats. Cover and blend till reduced to a powder. Transfer to a small bowl. Repeat with the remaining oats, ½ cup at a time. (You should have about 1½ cups of oat flour.) Set oat flour aside.

🍂 In a large mixing bowl beat margarine or butter with an electric mixer on medium to high speed about 30 seconds or till softened.

🍂 Add about *half* of the all-purpose flour to the margarine. Then add the sugar, brown sugar, eggs, orange peel (if desired), baking soda, vanilla, cinnamon, and nutmeg. Beat till thoroughly combined, scraping the sides of bowl occasionally. Then beat or stir in oat flour and remaining all-purpose flour. Stir in raisins or dates and chopped walnuts.

🍂 Drop dough by rounded tablespoons 2 inches apart onto ungreased cookie sheets. Bake in a 375° oven for 8 to 10 minutes or till edges are lightly browned. Cool on cookie sheets for 1 minute. Remove cookies and cool on wire racks. Makes about 42.

Nutrition information per cookie: 119 calories, 2 g protein, 17 g carbohydrate, 6 g fat (1 g saturated), 10 mg cholesterol, 63 mg sodium, 88 mg potassium.

17

Yummy! Savor creamy peanut butter sandwiched between layers of oatmeal, then topped with chocolate.

Pictured on the cover.

Chocolate-Peanut Butter Bars

　2　cups quick-cooking rolled oats
1¾　cups packed brown sugar
　1　cup all-purpose flour
　½　cup whole wheat flour
　1　teaspoon baking powder
　½　teaspoon baking soda
　1　cup margarine *or* butter
　½　cup chopped peanuts
　2　cups semisweet chocolate pieces
　1　beaten egg
　1　14-ounce can (1¼ cups) *sweetened condensed* milk
　⅓　cup creamy peanut butter

🐢 For crumb mixture, in a very large mixing bowl stir together the rolled oats, brown sugar, all-purpose flour, whole wheat flour, baking powder, and baking soda. Using a pastry blender, cut in the margarine or butter till mixture resembles fine crumbs. Stir in the chopped peanuts.

🐢 For topping, stir together *1¾ cups* of the crumb mixture and the chocolate pieces. Set topping aside.

🐢 For crust, stir the egg into the remaining crumb mixture. Press mixture into the bottom of an ungreased 15x10x1-inch baking pan. Bake in a 350° oven for 15 minutes.

🐢 For filling, stir together the sweetened condensed milk and peanut butter till well combined. Carefully pour the peanut-butter mixture evenly over the partially baked crust. Sprinkle with the topping.

🐢 Bake in a 350° oven for 12 to 15 minutes more or till lightly browned around the edges. Cool in pan on a wire rack. Cut into bars. Makes 48.

Nutrition information per bar: 179 calories, 3 g protein, 24 g carbohydrate, 9 g fat (2 g saturated), 8 mg cholesterol, 86 mg sodium, 137 mg potassium.

A great bar to have ready and waiting in the freezer. To freeze, wrap the cooled bars in moisture- and vaporproof-wrap and freeze for up to 6 months. To serve, remove wrap and thaw at room temperature about 2 hours.

Oatmeal-Caramel Bars

1	cup margarine *or* butter
2½	cups all-purpose flour
2	cups packed brown sugar
2	eggs
2	teaspoons vanilla
1	teaspoon baking soda
3	cups quick-cooking rolled oats
1	6-ounce package (1 cup) semisweet chocolate pieces
½	cup chopped walnuts *or* pecans
24	vanilla caramels (7 ounces)
2	tablespoons milk

🐢 In a large mixing bowl beat the margarine or butter with an electric mixer on medium to high speed about 30 seconds or till softened. Add about *1 cup* of the flour to the margarine. Then add the brown sugar, eggs, vanilla, and baking soda. Beat till thoroughly combined, scraping sides of bowl occasionally. Beat in the remaining flour. Stir in the rolled oats.

🐢 For crust, press *two-thirds* (about 3⅓ cups) of the oat mixture into the bottom of an ungreased 15x10x1-inch baking pan. Sprinkle with the chocolate pieces and nuts.

🐢 In a medium saucepan combine the caramels and milk. Cook and stir over low heat till the caramels are melted. Drizzle the caramel mixture over the chocolate and nuts. Drop the remaining oat mixture by rounded teaspoons on top of the caramel layer.

🐢 Bake in a 350° oven about 25 minutes or till top is lightly browned. Cool in pan on a wire rack. Cut into bars. Makes 60.

Nutrition information per bar: 109 calories, 1 g protein, 16 g carbohydrate, 5 g fat (1 g saturated), 7 mg cholesterol, 63 mg sodium, 56 mg potassium.

Down-to-earth, yet heavenly! You'll love the easy preparation and the luscious flavor of this brownie variation.

Brickle Bars

½ **cup margarine** *or* **butter**
2 **squares (2 ounces) unsweetened chocolate**
1 **cup sugar**
2 **eggs**
1 **teaspoon vanilla**
¾ **cup all-purpose flour**
¾ **cup almond brickle pieces**
½ **cup miniature semisweet chocolate pieces**

In a medium saucepan melt the margarine or butter and chocolate over low heat, stirring frequently. Remove from heat. Add the sugar, eggs, and vanilla. Using a wooden spoon, *lightly* beat just till combined (*don't overbeat* or brownies will rise too high, then fall). Stir in the flour.

Spread batter into a greased 8x8x2-inch baking pan. Sprinkle with almond brickle pieces and chocolate pieces. Bake in a 350° oven for 30 minutes. Cool in pan on a wire rack. Cut into bars. Makes 16.

Nutrition information per bar: 75 calories, 0 g protein, 10 g carbohydrate, 4 g fat (2 g saturated), 9 mg cholesterol, 19 mg sodium, 24 mg potassium.

If you like, for a whole wheat version of this decadent bar, substitute whole wheat flour for 1 cup of the all-purpose flour.

Chocolate Revel Bars

  1 **cup margarine** *or* **butter, softened**
2½ **cups all-purpose flour**
  2 **cups packed brown sugar**
  2 **eggs**
  2 **teaspoons vanilla**
  1 **teaspoon baking soda**
  3 **cups quick-cooking rolled oats**
1½ **cups semisweet chocolate pieces**
  1 **14-ounce can (1¼ cups)** *sweetened* **condensed** **milk**
  2 **tablespoons margarine** *or* **butter**
  ½ **cup chopped walnuts** *or* **pecans**
  2 **teaspoons vanilla**

🐟 In a very large mixing bowl beat the 1 cup margarine or butter with an electric mixer on medium to high speed about 30 seconds or till softened. Add about *half* of the flour to the margarine. Then add the brown sugar, eggs, 2 teaspoons vanilla, and baking soda. Beat till thoroughly combined, scraping the sides of the bowl occasionally. Beat in the remaining flour. Stir in the rolled oats. Set the oat mixture aside.

🐟 For filling, in a medium saucepan heat chocolate pieces, sweetened condensed milk, and the 2 tablespoons margarine or butter over low heat till chocolate is just melted, stirring occasionally. Remove from heat. Stir in the walnuts or pecans and 2 teaspoons vanilla.
🐟 For crust, press *two-thirds* (about 3⅓ cups) of the oat mixture into the bottom of an ungreased 15x10x1-inch baking pan. Spread the chocolate mixture over crust. Drop the remaining oat mixture by rounded teaspoons on top of chocolate layer.
🐟 Bake in a 350° oven about 25 minutes or till the top is lightly browned. (Chocolate mixture will still look moist.) Cool in pan on a wire rack. Cut into bars. Makes 60.

Nutrition information per bar: 149 calories, 2 g protein, 21 g carbohydrate, 6 g fat (1 g saturated), 10 mg cholesterol, 70 mg sodium, 100 mg potassium.

The buttermilk makes these cakelike brownies pleasingly tangy.

*B*uttermilk Brownies

> 2 **cups all-purpose flour**
> 2 **cups sugar**
> 1 **teaspoon baking soda**
> ¼ **teaspoon salt**
> 1 **cup margarine *or* butter**
> 1 **cup water**
> ⅓ **cup unsweetened cocoa powder**
> 2 **eggs**
> ½ **cup buttermilk *or* sour milk**
> 1½ **teaspoons vanilla**
> ¼ **cup margarine *or* butter**
> 3 **tablespoons unsweetened cocoa powder**
> 3 **tablespoons buttermilk *or* sour milk**
> 2¼ **cups sifted powdered sugar**
> ½ **teaspoon vanilla**
> ¾ **cup coarsely chopped pecans (optional)**

❧ In a large mixing bowl stir together the flour, sugar, baking soda, and salt. Set flour mixture aside.

❧ In a saucepan combine 1 cup margarine or butter, water, and ⅓ cup cocoa powder. Bring just to boiling, stirring constantly.

❧ Remove from heat. Add chocolate mixture to flour mixture. Beat with an electric mixer on medium to high speed till thoroughly combined. Add the eggs, ½ cup buttermilk or sour milk, and 1½ teaspoons vanilla. Beat for 1 minute more (batter will be thin).

❧ Pour batter into a greased 15x10x1-inch baking pan. Bake in a 350° oven about 25 minutes or till a wooden toothpick inserted near the center comes out clean.

❧ Meanwhile, for frosting, in a saucepan combine the ¼ cup margarine or butter, 3 tablespoons cocoa powder, and 3 tablespoons buttermilk or sour milk. Bring to boiling. Remove from heat. Add the powdered sugar and ½ teaspoon vanilla. Beat till smooth. If desired, stir in pecans. Pour warm frosting over *warm* brownies, spreading evenly. Cool in pan on a wire rack. Cut into bars. Makes 36.

Nutrition information per bar: 156 calories, 1 g protein, 23 g carbohydrate, 7 g fat (1 g saturated), 12 mg cholesterol, 120 mg sodium, 21 mg potassium.

A square malt? Put away
your straw and try these
bars for a scrumptious
snack.

Chocolate Malt Bars

1¼ **cups all-purpose flour**
 1 **teaspoon baking powder**
 ⅓ **cup margarine** *or* **butter, softened**
 ½ **cup sugar**
 1 **egg**
 ½ **cup instant malted milk powder**
 ¼ **cup milk**
 1 **teaspoon vanilla**
 1 **cup malted milk balls, coarsely**
    chopped
    Quick Fudge Frosting (optional)
 ⅓ **cup malted milk balls, coarsely**
    chopped (optional)

🍂 In a small mixing bowl stir together flour
and baking powder. Set aside.

🍂 In a large mixing bowl beat the margarine
or butter with an electric mixer on medium to
high speed about 30 seconds or till softened.
Add sugar and beat till fluffy. Add the egg,
malted milk powder, milk, and vanilla. Beat for
2 to 3 minutes or till thoroughly combined,
scraping the sides of the bowl occasionally.

🍂 With the mixer on low speed, gradually
add the flour mixture to the margarine
mixture, beating for 2 to 3 minutes or till
thoroughly combined. Fold in the 1 cup malted
milk balls.

🍂 Spread the mixture into a greased 9x9x2-
inch baking pan. Bake in a 350° oven for 25 to
30 minutes or till a wooden toothpick inserted
near the center comes out clean. Cool in pan
on a wire rack. If desired, frost cooled bars
with Quick Fudge Frosting and sprinkle with
the ⅓ cup milk balls. Makes 16 bars.

Quick Fudge Frosting: In a medium mixing
bowl stir together 2½ cups *sifted powdered sugar*
and ¼ cup *unsweetened cocoa powder*. Add ¼ cup
margarine or butter, 3 tablespoons *boiling water*,
and ½ teaspoon *vanilla*. Beat with an electric
mixer on low speed till combined. Beat on
medium speed for 1 minute more. Cool for 20
to 30 minutes or till spreading consistency.

Nutrition information per bar: 141 calories,
2 g protein, 21 g carbohydrate, 5 g fat (1 g saturated),
15 mg cholesterol, 92 mg sodium, 81 mg potassium.

A light sifting of powdered sugar over the top of these brownies is a tasty alternative to the frosting.

Orange Brownies

½ **cup margarine** *or* **butter**
2 **squares (2 ounces) unsweetened chocolate**
1 **cup sugar**
2 **eggs**
1 **teaspoon finely shredded orange peel**
1 **teaspoon vanilla**
¾ **cup all-purpose flour**
½ **cup chopped walnuts** *or* **pecans**
Orange-Fudge Frosting

🐢 In a medium saucepan melt margarine or butter and chocolate over low heat, stirring constantly. Remove from heat. Add the sugar, eggs, orange peel, and vanilla. Using a wooden spoon, *lightly* beat just till combined *(don't overbeat* or brownies will rise too high, then fall). Stir in the flour and walnuts or pecans.
🐢 Spread batter into a greased 8x8x2-inch baking pan. Bake in a 350° oven for 30 minutes. Cool in pan on a wire rack. Spread Orange-Fudge Frosting over cooled brownies. If desired, score frosting with tines of fork. Cut into bars. Makes 24.

Orange-Fudge Frosting: In a medium mixing bowl stir together 1½ cups sifted *powdered sugar* and 3 tablespoons *unsweetened cocoa powder*. Add 3 tablespoons softened *margarine or butter*, 2 tablespoons very hot *water,* ½ teaspoon finely shredded *orange peel,* and ½ teaspoon *vanilla.* Beat with electric mixer on low speed till combined. Beat on medium speed for 1 minute more.

Nutrition information per bar: 151 calories, 2 g protein, 19 g carbohydrate, 9 g fat (1 g saturated), 18 mg cholesterol, 67 mg sodium, 45 mg potassium.

Fudge Brownies: Prepare Orange Brownies as directed at left, *except* omit the orange peel in the brownies and in the frosting.

Nutrition information per bar: 151 calories, 2 g protein, 19 g carbohydrate, 9 g fat (1 g saturated), 18 mg cholesterol, 67 mg sodium, 45 mg potassium.

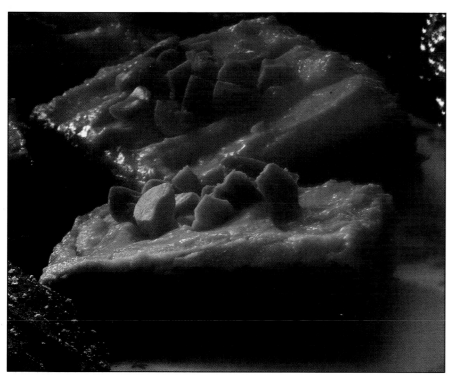

Creamy peanut butter frosting complements the spiciness of these cakey applesauce bars.

Old-Fashioned Applesauce Bars

½ cup all-purpose flour
½ cup sugar
¼ cup whole wheat flour
¾ teaspoon baking powder
½ teaspoon ground cinnamon
¼ teaspoon baking soda
⅛ teaspoon salt
⅛ teaspoon ground cloves
⅓ cup applesauce
⅓ cup cooking oil
2 beaten eggs
Peanut Butter and Cream Cheese Frosting
¼ cup finely chopped peanuts

🐢 In a medium mixing bowl stir together the all-purpose flour, sugar, whole wheat flour, baking powder, cinnamon, baking soda, salt, and cloves. Add the applesauce, cooking oil, and eggs. Stir till thoroughly combined. Spread the batter into an ungreased 13x9x2-inch baking pan.

🐢 Bake in a 350° oven about 15 minutes or till a wooden toothpick inserted near the center comes out clean. Cool in pan on a wire rack. Spread Peanut Butter and Cream Cheese Frosting over the cooled bars. Sprinkle with peanuts. Cut into bars. Store, covered, in the refrigerator. Makes 36.

Peanut Butter and Cream Cheese Frosting:
In large mixing bowl beat one 3-ounce package *cream cheese* and ¼ cup creamy *peanut butter* with an electric mixer on medium to high speed till light and fluffy. Gradually add 1 cup sifted *powdered sugar*, beating well. Beat in 2 tablespoons *milk*. Gradually beat in about 1⅓ cups additional sifted *powdered sugar* to make of spreading consistency.

Nutrition information per bar: 92 calories, 2 g protein, 12 g carbohydrate, 4 g fat (1 g saturated), 15 mg cholesterol, 39 mg sodium, 34 mg potassium.

Dress up these bars by drizzling the icing in a decorative pattern.

Butterscotch-Allspice Bars

      1 **cup all-purpose flour**
      3 **tablespoons sugar**
    ⅓ **cup margarine *or* butter**
    ½ **cup all-purpose flour**
    ½ **teaspoon baking powder**
    ½ **teaspoon ground allspice**
    ¼ **teaspoon salt**
    ¼ **cup margarine *or* butter**
      1 **cup packed brown sugar**
      1 **beaten egg**
      1 **teaspoon vanilla**
      1 **cup chopped pecans**
         Powdered Sugar Icing

❧ For crust, in a medium mixing bowl stir together the 1 cup flour and 3 tablespoons sugar. Using a pastry blender, cut in the ⅓ cup margarine or butter till mixture resembles fine crumbs. Press the crumb mixture into the bottom of an ungreased 9x9x2-inch baking pan. Bake in 350° oven for 10 minutes.

❧ Meanwhile, in a small bowl stir together ½ cup flour, baking powder, allspice, and salt. Set aside.

❧ In a medium saucepan melt ¼ cup margarine or butter. Stir in the brown sugar. Remove from heat. Add the flour-baking powder mixture, egg, and vanilla. Stir till thoroughly mixed. Stir in pecans. Pour batter over the warm, partially baked crust.

❧ Bake in 350° oven for 20 to 25 minutes more or till a wooden toothpick inserted near center comes out clean. Cool in pan on a wire rack. Drizzle with Powdered Sugar Icing. Cut into bars. Makes 32.

Powdered Sugar Icing: In a small bowl stir together 1 cup sifted *powdered sugar*, ¼ teaspoon *vanilla*, and enough *milk* (about 1 tablespoon) to make of drizzling consistency.

Nutrition information per bar: 117 calories, 1 g protein, 16 g carbohydrate, 6 g fat (1 g saturated), 7 mg cholesterol, 64 mg sodium, 47 mg potassium.

The flavor of carrot cake and the moistness of zucchini bars come together in these vegetable-rich cookies.

Carrot and Zucchini Bars

1½ cups all-purpose flour
¾ cup packed brown sugar
1 teaspoon baking powder
½ teaspoon ground ginger
¼ teaspoon baking soda
2 slightly beaten eggs
1½ cups shredded carrot
1 medium zucchini, shredded (1 cup)
½ cup raisins
½ cup chopped walnuts *or* pecans
½ cup cooking oil
¼ cup honey
1 teaspoon vanilla
    Citrus-Cream Cheese Frosting

🐢 In a large mixing bowl stir together the flour, brown sugar, baking powder, ginger, and baking soda. Set aside.

🐢 In a medium mixing bowl stir together the eggs, carrot, zucchini, raisins, walnuts or pecans, cooking oil, honey, and vanilla. Add the carrot mixture to flour mixture. Using a wooden spoon, stir just till combined.

🐢 Spread the batter into an ungreased 13x9x2-inch baking pan. Bake in a 350° oven about 25 minutes or till a wooden toothpick inserted near the center comes out clean. Cool in pan on a wire rack. Spread the Citrus-Cream Cheese Frosting over cooled bars. Cut into bars. Store, covered, in refrigerator. Makes 36.

Citrus-Cream Cheese Frosting: In a small mixing bowl combine one 8-ounce container *light cream cheese product,* ½ cup sifted *powdered sugar,* 2 tablespoons *orange juice,* and 1 tablespoon finely shredded *lemon peel or orange peel.* Beat with an electric mixer on medium speed till light and fluffy.

Nutrition information per bar: 112 calories, 2 g protein, 15 g carbohydrate, 6 g fat (1 g saturated), 15 mg cholesterol, 58 mg sodium, 85 mg potassium.

Combine the tangy flavors of cranberries and lemon peel to give these quick-to-fix bars an unbeatable taste.

Cranberry Bars

1½ **cups all-purpose flour**
1½ **cups quick-cooking rolled oats**
¾ **cup packed brown sugar**
1 **teaspoon finely shredded lemon peel**
¼ **teaspoon baking soda**
¾ **cup margarine *or* butter, melted**
1 **16-ounce can whole cranberry sauce**
¼ **cup finely chopped pecans *or* walnuts**

🐢 In a large mixing bowl stir together the flour, rolled oats, brown sugar, lemon peel, and baking soda. Stir in the melted margarine or butter and mix thoroughly.

🐢 For topping, reserve *1 cup* of the oat mixture. Set aside.

🐢 For crust, press the remaining oat mixture into the bottom of an ungreased 13x9x2-inch baking pan. Bake in a 350° oven for 20 minutes.

🐢 Carefully spread the cranberry sauce evenly over the partially baked crust. Stir the pecans or walnuts into the reserved topping. Sprinkle over cranberry sauce. Lightly pat topping into sauce. Bake in a 350° oven for 25 to 30 minutes more or till top is lightly browned. Cool in pan on a wire rack. Cut into bars. Makes 24.

Nutrition information per bar: 408 calories, 2 g protein, 88 g carbohydrate, 7 g fat (1 g saturated), 0 mg cholesterol, 131 mg sodium, 105 mg potassium.

Pumpkin Bars

2 cups all-purpose flour
1½ cups sugar
2 teaspoons baking powder
2 teaspoons ground cinnamon
1 teaspoon baking soda
¼ teaspoon salt
¼ teaspoon ground cloves
1 16-ounce can pumpkin
1 cup cooking oil
4 beaten eggs
1 cup chopped walnuts (optional)
  Cream Cheese Frosting *or* powdered
    sugar

In a large mixing bowl stir together the flour, sugar, baking powder, cinnamon, baking soda, salt, and cloves. Stir in the pumpkin, cooking oil, and eggs till thoroughly combined. If desired, stir in the walnuts.

Spread batter into an ungreased 15x10x1-inch baking pan.

Bake in a 350° oven for 25 to 30 minutes or till a wooden toothpick inserted near the center comes out clean. Cool in pan on a wire rack. Frost with Cream Cheese Frosting or sift powdered sugar over top. Cut into bars. Store, covered, in the refrigerator. Makes 48.

Cream Cheese Frosting: In a medium mixing bowl beat one 3-ounce package *cream cheese,* ¼ cup *margarine or butter,* and 1 teaspoon *vanilla* with an electric mixer on medium to high speed till light and fluffy. Gradually add 1 cup sifted *powdered sugar,* beating well. Gradually beat in about 1¼ cups additional sifted *powdered sugar* to make of spreading consistency.

Nutrition information per bar: 118 calories, 1 g protein, 15 g carbohydrate, 6 g fat (1 g saturated), 20 mg cholesterol, 56 mg sodium, 33 mg potassium.

A tasty crumb crust topped with a zippy lemon custard.

Lemon Bars

⅓ **cup margarine *or* butter**
¼ **cup sugar**
1 **cup all-purpose flour**
2 **eggs**
¾ **cup sugar**
2 **tablespoons all-purpose flour**
2 **teaspoons finely shredded lemon peel (set aside)**
3 **tablespoons lemon juice**
¼ **teaspoon baking powder**
⅛ **teaspoon salt**
　 Powdered sugar (optional)

❧ For crust, in a medium mixing bowl beat margarine or butter with an electric mixer on medium to high speed about 30 seconds or till softened. Add ¼ cup sugar. Beat till thoroughly combined. Then beat in 1 cup flour till mixture resembles fine crumbs. Press mixture into the bottom of an ungreased 8x8x2-inch baking pan. Bake in a 350° oven for 15 minutes.

❧ Meanwhile, for lemon mixture, in the same mixing bowl beat eggs with an electric mixer on medium speed just till foamy. Add ¾ cup sugar, 2 tablespoons flour, lemon juice, baking powder, and salt. Beat on medium speed about 3 minutes more or till slightly thickened. Stir in the lemon peel. Pour the lemon mixture over the partially baked crust.

❧ Bake in a 350° oven for 20 to 25 minutes more or till lightly browned around edges and the center is set. Cool in pan on a wire rack. If desired, sift with powdered sugar. Cut into bars. Store, covered, in refrigerator. Makes 20.

Nutrition information per bar: 95 calories, 1 g protein, 15 g carbohydrate, 4 g fat (1 g saturated), 21 mg cholesterol, 59 mg sodium, 18 mg potassium.

Coconut-Lemon Bars: Prepare Lemon Bars as directed at left, *except* increase the baking powder to *½ teaspoon* and stir 1 cup flaked *coconut* into the lemon mixture.

Nutrition information per bar: 112 calories, 1 g protein, 16 g carbohydrate, 5 g fat (2 g saturated), 21 mg cholesterol, 63 mg sodium, 30 mg potassium.

When you yearn for something wonderfully delicious, stir together a batch of these quick bars— no mixer needed.

Macadamia-Coconut Bars

1¼ cups all-purpose flour
  3 tablespoons packed brown sugar
  ½ cup margarine *or* butter
  2 slightly beaten eggs
  ½ cup sugar
  ¼ teaspoon ground nutmeg
  ⅛ teaspoon ground cinnamon
  ⅔ cup chopped macadamia nuts *or* chopped toasted almonds
  ½ cup light corn syrup
  ½ cup flaked coconut
  2 tablespoons margarine *or* butter, melted
  ½ teaspoon vanilla

🐾 For crust, in a medium mixing bowl stir together the flour and brown sugar. Using a pastry blender, cut in ½ cup margarine or butter till mixture resembles coarse crumbs.

Press the crumb mixture into the bottom of an ungreased 11x7x1½-inch baking pan. Bake in a 375° oven for 20 minutes.

🐾 Meanwhile, in another mixing bowl stir together the eggs, sugar, nutmeg, and cinnamon. Add the macadamia nuts or almonds, corn syrup, coconut, melted margarine or butter, and vanilla. Stir just till the mixture is combined. Pour nut mixture over the partially baked crust, spreading evenly.

🐾 Bake in a 375° oven for 15 to 20 minutes or till the center appears set. Cool slightly in the pan on a wire rack. Cut into 1½-inch squares. Cool completely. Store, covered, in the refrigerator. Makes 24.

Nutrition information per bar: 146 calories, 1 g protein, 16 g carbohydrate, 9 g fat (2 g saturated), 18 mg cholesterol, 67 mg sodium, 38 mg potassium.

31

Finely chop the walnuts to make the dough easy to slice.

Oatmeal-Nut Crisps

½ **cup shortening**
½ **cup margarine *or* butter**
1½ **cups all-purpose flour**
1 **cup sugar**
1 **cup packed brown sugar**
2 **eggs**
1½ **teaspoons ground cinnamon**
1 **teaspoon baking soda**
1 **teaspoon vanilla**
½ **teaspoon salt**
3 **cups quick-cooking rolled oats**
½ **cup finely chopped black walnuts *or* walnuts**

✿ In a large mixing bowl beat shortening and margarine or butter with an electric mixer on medium to high speed about 30 seconds or till softened. Add about *half* of the flour to the shortening mixture. Then add the sugar, brown sugar, eggs, cinnamon, baking soda, vanilla, and salt. Beat till thoroughly combined, scraping sides of bowl occasionally. Then beat or stir in the remaining flour. Stir in rolled oats and finely chopped nuts.

✿ Shape dough into two 10-inch rolls. Wrap each in waxed paper or plastic wrap. Chill for 4 to 48 hours.

✿ Cut dough into ¼-inch-thick slices. Place 1 inch apart onto ungreased cookie sheets. Bake in a 375° oven for 7 to 9 minutes or till edges are lightly browned. Cool on the cookie sheets for 1 minute. Remove cookies and cool on wire racks. Makes about 70.

Nutrition information per cookie: 77 calories, 1 g protein, 10 g carbohydrate, 4 g fat (1 g saturated), 6 mg cholesterol, 60 mg sodium, 33 mg potassium.

Slice-of-Orange Cookies

2⅓ cups all-purpose flour
  1 cup sugar
  ¾ cup margarine *or* butter, softened
  1 egg
  2 teaspoons finely shredded orange peel
  2 tablespoons orange juice
  1 teaspoon baking powder
  ¼ teaspoon salt
  ½ cup finely chopped almonds
     Decorator's Icing
  3 to 4 drops yellow food coloring
       (optional)
  1 drop red food coloring (optional)

🐢 In a large mixing bowl combine flour, sugar, margarine or butter, egg, orange peel, orange juice, baking powder, and salt. Beat with an electric mixer about 30 seconds or till combined. Beat on medium speed for 2 minutes, scraping sides of bowl frequently.
🐢 Shape into two 7-inch rolls. Roll in finely chopped almonds. Flatten one side of each roll. Wrap each in waxed paper or plastic wrap. Chill for 4 to 48 hours.
🐢 Cut dough into ¼-inch-thick slices. Place 1 inch apart onto ungreased cookie sheets. Bake in a 375° oven for 10 to 12 minutes or till edges are lightly browned. Remove cookies and cool on wire racks. If desired, tint Decorator's Icing with yellow and red food coloring. Pipe icing in loops on each cookie to represent orange sections. Makes about 60.

Decorator's Icing: In a small mixing bowl combine 1 cup sifted *powdered sugar,* ½ teaspoon *vanilla,* and enough *light cream or milk* (about 1 tablespoon) to make icing of piping consistency.

Nutrition information per cookie: 63 calories, 1 g protein, 9 g carbohydrate, 3 g fat (0 g saturated), 4 mg cholesterol, 42 mg sodium, 17 mg potassium.

If you wish, frost these citrus slices to resemble orange sections.

Pictured on the cover.

33

To keep all of your cookies nice and round, rotate the rolls frequently while you're slicing.

Maple-Nut Slices

½ cup shortening
½ cup margarine *or* butter
3 cups all-purpose flour
1¼ cups packed brown sugar
1 egg
2 tablespoons milk
1½ teaspoons maple flavoring
½ teaspoon baking soda
¼ teaspoon salt
1 slightly beaten egg white
1 cup finely chopped toasted pecans
Powdered Sugar Icing

In a large mixing bowl beat shortening and margarine or butter with an electric mixer on medium to high speed about 30 seconds or till softened. Add about *1 cup* of the flour to the shortening mixture. Then add the brown sugar, egg, milk, maple flavoring, baking soda, and salt. Beat till thoroughly combined, scraping the sides of bowl occasionally. Then beat or stir in the remaining flour.

Shape dough into three 8-inch rolls. Brush rolls with egg white, then roll in chopped pecans. Wrap each in waxed paper or plastic wrap. Chill for 4 to 48 hours.

Cut dough into ¼-inch-thick slices. Place 1 inch apart onto ungreased cookie sheets. Bake in a 375° oven about 8 minutes or till edges are firm. Remove cookies and cool on wire racks. Drizzle with Powdered Sugar Icing. Makes about 90.

Powdered Sugar Icing: In a small mixing bowl combine 1 cup sifted *powdered sugar,* ¼ teaspoon *vanilla,* and enough *milk* (1 to 2 tablespoons) to make icing of drizzling consistency.

Nutrition information per cookie: 58 calories, 1 g protein, 7 g carbohydrate, 3 g fat (1 g saturated), 2 mg cholesterol, 25 mg sodium, 22 mg potassium.

Date Pinwheel Cookies

1 8-ounce package (1⅓ cups) pitted whole dates, snipped
⅓ cup sugar
2 tablespoons lemon juice
½ teaspoon vanilla
½ cup shortening
½ cup margarine *or* butter
3 cups all-purpose flour
½ cup sugar
½ cup packed brown sugar
1 egg
3 tablespoons milk
1 teaspoon vanilla
½ teaspoon baking soda

For filling, in a medium saucepan combine dates, ⅓ cup sugar, and ½ cup *water*. Bring to boiling; reduce heat. Cook and stir about 2 minutes or till thick. Stir in lemon juice and the ½ teaspoon vanilla; cool.

In a mixing bowl beat shortening and margarine or butter with an electric mixer on medium to high speed for 30 seconds. Add about *half* of the flour. Then add the ½ cup sugar, the brown sugar, egg, milk, 1 teaspoon vanilla, baking soda, and ¼ teaspoon *salt.* Beat till combined. Beat in remaining flour. Cover and chill about 1 hour or till easy to handle.

Divide in half. Roll *each* half of dough between waxed paper into a 12x10-inch rectangle. Spread with filling. From a long side, roll up each half jelly-roll style. Moisten and pinch edges to seal. Wrap each in waxed paper or plastic wrap. Chill for 4 to 48 hours.

Cut into ¼-inch slices. Place 1 inch apart onto greased cookie sheets. Bake in a 375° oven for 10 to 12 minutes or till edges are lightly browned. Cool on wire racks. Makes about 72.

Nutrition information per cookie: 66 calories, 1 g protein, 10 g carbohydrate, 3 g fat (1 g saturated), 3 mg cholesterol, 19 mg sodium, 35 mg potassium.

A pretty gift cookie for a special friend.

Red Raspberry Twirls

½ **cup margarine *or* butter**
2¾ **cups all-purpose flour**
1 **cup sugar**
1 **egg**
3 **tablespoons milk**
½ **teaspoon baking powder**
¼ **teaspoon almond extract (optional)**
½ **cup seedless red raspberry jam**
1½ **teaspoons cornstarch**
½ **cup toasted almonds, ground**

❧ In a mixing bowl beat margarine or butter with an electric mixer on medium to high speed about 30 seconds or till softened. Add *1 cup* of the flour to the margarine. Then add the sugar, egg, milk, baking powder, and, if desired, almond extract. Beat till combined. Then beat or stir in the remaining flour. Cover and chill about 1 hour or till easy to handle.

❧ For filling, in a small saucepan combine jam and cornstarch. Cook and stir till thickened and bubbly. Cook and stir for 1 minute more. Stir in ground almonds. Cover and set aside to cool slightly.

❧ Divide dough in half. Roll *each* half between waxed paper into a 12x8-inch rectangle. Spread with filling. From a short side, roll up each half jelly-roll style, removing waxed paper as you roll. Moisten and pinch edges to seal. Wrap each in waxed paper or plastic wrap. Chill for 4 to 48 hours.

❧ Cut dough into ¼-inch-thick slices. Place 2 inches apart onto greased, *foil-lined* cookie sheets. Bake in a 375° oven for 9 to 11 minutes or till edges are firm and bottoms are lightly browned. Remove cookies and cool on wire racks. Makes about 60.

Nutrition information per cookie: 58 calories, 1 g protein, 9 g carbohydrate, 2 g fat (0 g saturated), 4 mg cholesterol, 22 mg sodium, 16 mg potassium.

Selecting Margarines

❧ If you prefer to use margarine in your cookies, select one that is not a spread, diet, or soft-style margarine product. And remember, if you choose margarine that's 100 percent corn oil, your dough will be softer than dough made from other margarines. For sliced or shaped cookie dough, you'll need to chill the dough in the freezer instead of the refrigerator. For cutout cookie dough, refrigerate the dough at least 5 hours before rolling it out.

Sliced Cookie Dough

Attention busy bakers. Save time by making a trio of different cookies from one dough.

¾ **cup shortening**
¾ **cup margarine *or* butter**
4½ **cups all-purpose flour**
1½ **cups sugar**
1 **egg**
3 **tablespoons milk**
1 **egg yolk**
1½ **teaspoons vanilla**
¼ **teaspoon baking soda**
¼ **teaspoon salt**

🍂 In a large mixing bowl beat shortening and margarine or butter with an electric mixer on medium to high speed about 30 seconds or till softened. Add about *half* of the flour to the shortening mixture. Then add the sugar, whole egg, milk, egg yolk, vanilla, baking soda, and salt. Beat till thoroughly combined, scraping sides of bowl occasionally. Then beat or stir in the remaining flour.

🍂 Divide dough into 3 portions. Use dough to make Lemon-Almond Tea Cookies, Choco-Candy Cookies, and Cherry-Pecan Rounds.

36

Lemon-Almond Tea Cookies

Pucker up for a sweet-tart taste! Pictured on the cover and on opposite page.

⅓ **of a recipe Sliced Cookie Dough (see recipe, opposite)**
2 **teaspoons finley shredded lemon peel**
1 **teaspoon almond extract**
¼ **cup margarine** *or* **butter**
2 **cups sifted powdered sugar**
1 **tablespoon milk**
1 **teaspoon lemon juice**
   Few drops almond extract
½ **cup toasted, sliced almonds**

❧ In a medium mixing bowl combine the ⅓ recipe cookie dough, lemon peel, and the 1 teaspoon almond extract. Using a wooden spoon, mix till thoroughly combined.

❧ Shape dough into an 8-inch roll. Wrap in waxed paper or plastic wrap. Chill dough for 4 to 48 hours.

❧ Cut dough into ¼-inch-thick slices. Place about 2 inches apart onto ungreased cookie sheets. Bake in a 375° oven for 8 to 10 minutes or till edges are firm and bottoms are lightly browned. Remove cookies and cool on wire racks.

❧ For frosting, in a small mixing bowl beat the margarine or butter with an electric mixer on medium to high speed about 30 seconds or till softened. Add *half* of the powdered sugar, beating till combined. Beat in the milk, lemon juice, and few drops almond extract. Gradually beat in the remaining powdered sugar till frosting is smooth.

❧ Spread about *1 teaspoon* of the frosting atop each cookie. Sprinkle with sliced almonds. Makes about 32.

Nutrition information per cookie: 109 calories, 1 g protein, 14 g carbohydrate, 6 g fat (1 g saturated), 5 mg cholesterol, 43 mg sodium, 25 mg potassium.

Choco-Candy Cookies

Turn an ordinary occasion into a special one with these festive-looking treats! Pictured on the cover and on page 36.

⅓ **of a recipe Sliced Cookie Dough (see recipe, page 36)**
2 **squares (2 ounces) semisweet chocolate, melted and cooled**
2 **teaspoons milk**
Candy-and-milk-chocolate-covered peanuts *or* almonds

🐦 In a medium mixing bowl combine the ⅓ recipe cookie dough, melted and cooled chocolate, and milk. Using a wooden spoon, mix till thoroughly combined.

🐦 Shape dough into an 8-inch roll. Wrap in waxed paper or plastic wrap. Chill dough for 4 to 48 hours.

🐦 Cut dough into ¾-inch-thick slices. Cut *each* slice into *quarters*. Shape each quarter into a ball. Place 2 inches apart onto ungreased cookie sheets.

🐦 Bake in a 375° oven for 8 to 10 minutes or till tops look dry. *Immediately* press a candy-and-milk-chocolate-covered peanut or almond gently and evenly into each cookie. Remove cookies; cool on wire racks. Makes about 48.

Nutrition information per cookie: 55 calories, 1 g protein, 7 g carbohydrate, 3 g fat (0 g saturated), 3 mg cholesterol, 19 mg sodium, 18 mg potassium.

Cherry-Pecan Rounds

To vary the flavor and the appearance, roll the dough in coconut instead of the finely chopped nuts. Pictured on the cover and on page 36.

⅓ **of a recipe Sliced Cookie Dough (see recipe, page 36)**
¾ **cup maraschino cherries, drained and finely chopped**
Few drops red food coloring (optional)
½ **cup finely chopped pecans *or* walnuts**

🐦 In a medium mixing bowl combine the ⅓ recipe cookie dough, maraschino cherries, and, if desired, red food coloring. Using a wooden spoon, mix till thoroughly combined.

🐦 Shape dough into a 10-inch roll. Roll the dough in the finely chopped nuts until coated. Wrap in waxed paper or plastic wrap. Chill for 4 to 48 hours.

🐦 Cut dough into ¼-inch-thick slices. Place 2 inches apart onto ungreased cookie sheets. Bake in a 375° oven for 8 to 10 minutes or till edges are firm and bottoms are lightly browned. Cool on wire racks. Makes about 36.

Nutrition information per cookie: 102 calories, 1 g protein, 14 g carbohydrate, 5 g fat (1 g saturated), 4 mg cholesterol, 38 mg sodium, 34 mg potassium.

Like cotton candy, these cream cheese-filled cookies will simply melt in your mouth.

*A*lmond Meringues

3 **egg whites**
¼ **teaspoon cream of tartar**
¼ **teaspoon almond extract**
1 **cup sugar**
1 **8-ounce container soft-style cream cheese with pineapple**
Fresh fruit *or* **preserves**

🍂 In a large mixing bowl let the egg whites stand at room temperature for 30 minutes. Meanwhile, line 2 large cookie sheets with parchment paper. Set aside.

🍂 Add the cream of tartar and almond extract to the egg whites. Beat with an electric mixer on medium speed till soft peaks form (tips curl). Gradually add sugar, *1 tablespoon* at a time, beating on high speed till stiff peaks form (tips stand straight) and sugar is *almost* dissolved.

🍂 Drop meringue mixture by tablespoons 2 inches apart onto the prepared cookie sheets. With the back of a spoon, make an indentation in the center of each, building up sides.

🍂 Bake in a 300° oven for 20 minutes. Turn off oven. Let cookies dry in oven with the door closed for 30 minutes. Peel cookies from paper. (If desired, store in an airtight container in a cool, dry place for up to 1 week.)

🍂 Just before serving, spoon a generous *teaspoon* of cream cheese into center of *each* meringue. Top with fruit or preserves. Serve immediately. Makes about 40.

Nutrition information per cookie: 38 calories, 0 g protein, 6 g carbohydrate, 2 g fat (1 g saturated), 5 mg cholesterol, 22 mg sodium, 19 mg potassium.

*N*o peeking is the key to the crispness of these snow white morsels. Once you turn the oven off, the oven door should remain closed so the cookies will dry properly.

*H*azelnut Meringues

  2 **egg whites**
 ½ **teaspoon vanilla**
 ¼ **teaspoon cream of tartar**
 ⅔ **cup sugar**
  2 **teaspoons hazelnut liqueur** *or*
       crème de cacao
 45 **whole hazelnuts (filberts)**
 ½ **cup milk chocolate pieces**
  2 **teaspoons shortening**

❧ In a small mixing bowl let the egg whites stand at room temperature for 30 minutes. Meanwhile, line a large cookie sheet with parchment paper. Set aside.

❧ Add the vanilla and cream of tartar to the egg whites. Beat with an electric mixer on medium speed till soft peaks form (tips curl). Gradually add sugar, *1 tablespoon* at a time, beating on high speed till stiff peaks form (tips stand straight) and sugar is *almost* dissolved. Gently fold in hazelnut liqueur or crème de cacao.

❧ Spoon meringue mixture into a decorating bag fitted with a large star tip (½-inch opening), filling the bag half full. Pipe 1½-inch-diameter stars about 1½ inches apart onto prepared cookie sheet, refilling the bag as necessary. Press a hazelnut into the center of each star.

❧ Bake in a 300° oven for 3 minutes. Turn off oven. Let cookies dry in oven with the door closed for 45 minutes or till crisp. Peel cookies from paper.

❧ In a small heavy saucepan melt the chocolate pieces and shortening over low heat, stirring occasionally. Dip the bottom of each meringue in chocolate. Using a knife, wipe excess chocolate off the bottom of each cookie. Place cookies, chocolate sides down, on waxed paper till chocolate is set. (If desired, store in an airtight container in a cool, dry place for up to 1 week.) Makes about 45.

Nutrition information per cookie: 35 calories, 0 g protein, 5 g carbohydrate, 2 g fat (0 g saturated), 0 mg cholesterol, 4 mg sodium, 16 mg potassium.

These crisp little cookies are really quite playful. But don't worry, they won't snap at you.

Snapper Cookies

¾ **cup margarine** *or* **butter**
¾ **cup brown sugar**
1 **egg**
1 **teaspoon vanilla**
2 **cups all-purpose flour**
2 **cups small pecan halves**
¾ **cup semisweet chocolate pieces**
2 **teaspoons shortening**

🐢 In a large mixing bowl beat the margarine or butter with an electric mixer on medium to high speed about 30 seconds or till softened. Add the brown sugar and beat till fluffy. Add the egg and vanilla. Beat till thoroughly combined, scraping the sides of the bowl occasionally. Then beat in the flour till well mixed.

🐢 Shape the dough into ¾-inch balls. Place about 2 inches apart onto ungreased cookie sheets. Tuck 3 or 4 small pecan halves under each ball. Slightly flatten balls.

🐢 Bake in a 375° oven for 9 to 10 minutes or till lightly browned on the bottoms. Remove cookies and cool on wire racks.

🐢 In a small heavy saucepan melt the chocolate pieces and shortening over low heat, stirring occasionally. Using a knife, swirl chocolate on the tops of the cookies. Makes about 42.

Nutrition information per cookie: 106 calories, 1 g protein, 9 g carbohydrate, 8 g fat (1 g saturated), 5 mg cholesterol, 41 mg sodium, 49 mg potassium.

41

🌿 Bake in a 325° oven for 25 to 30 minutes or till the bottom just starts to brown and the center is set. Cut the circle into wedges again while warm. Cool on the cookie sheet for 5 minutes. Remove cookies and cool on wire racks. Makes 16.

*Note: For strips or rounds, on a lightly floured surface, pat or roll dough to ½ inch thickness. Using a knife, cut into 2x1-inch strips; or, using a 1½-inch round cookie cutter, cut into rounds. Place 1 inch apart on an ungreased cookie sheet. Bake in a 325° oven for 20 to 25 minutes or till bottoms just start to brown. Remove cookies and cool on wire racks.

Nutrition information per cookie: 92 calories, 1 g protein, 9 g carbohydrate, 6 g fat (4 g saturated), 16 mg cholesterol, 59 mg sodium, 11 mg potassium.

Butter gives these scrumptious cookies their traditional rich flavor.

Shortbread

1¼ **cups all-purpose flour**
3 **tablespoons sugar**
½ **cup butter** (*not margarine*)

🌿 In a medium mixing bowl stir together the flour and sugar. Using a pastry blender, cut in the butter till the mixture resembles fine crumbs and starts to cling. Form the mixture into a ball and knead till smooth.

🌿 To make wedges,* on an ungreased cookie sheet pat or roll the dough into an 8-inch circle. Using your fingers, press to make a scalloped edge. With a knife, cut the circle into 16 pie-shape wedges. Leave wedges in the circle shape.

Lemon and Poppy Seed Shortbread: Prepare Shortbread as directed at left, *except* stir 1 tablespoon *poppy seed* into flour-sugar mixture and add 1 teaspoon finely shredded *lemon peel* with the butter.

Nutrition information per cookie: 95 calories, 1 g protein, 9 g carbohydrate, 6 g fat (4 g saturated), 16 mg cholesterol, 59 mg sodium, 15 mg potassium.

Butter-Pecan Shortbread: Prepare Shortbread as directed at left, *except* substitute *brown sugar* for the sugar. After cutting in butter, stir 2 tablespoons finely chopped *pecans* into the mixture. Sprinkle mixture with ½ teaspoon *vanilla.*

Nutrition information per cookie: 99 calories, 1 g protein, 10 g carbohydrate, 6 g fat (4 g saturated), 16 mg cholesterol, 60 mg sodium, 24 mg potassium.

*W*hole Wheat-Peanut Butter Blossoms

Package some of these chocolate-kiss-topped cookies for your valentine. Place them in a heart-shape box and deliver them with love.

1 cup all-purpose flour
¾ cup whole wheat flour
1 teaspoon baking powder
⅛ teaspoon baking soda
½ cup shortening
½ cup peanut butter
½ cup sugar
½ cup packed brown sugar
1 egg
2 tablespoons milk
1 teaspoon vanilla
½ cup chopped peanuts
    Sugar
    Milk chocolate kisses *or* stars

🐦 In a medium mixing bowl stir together the all-purpose flour, whole wheat flour, baking powder, and baking soda. Set aside.

🐦 In a large mixing bowl beat the shortening and peanut butter with an electric mixer on medium speed about 30 seconds. Add the ½ cup sugar and brown sugar and beat till fluffy. Then add the egg, milk, and vanilla. Beat till thoroughly combined, scraping the sides of the bowl occasionally. Gradually stir or beat in the flour mixture till thoroughly combined. Stir in the peanuts.

🐦 Shape dough into 1-inch balls. Roll the balls in sugar to coat. Place balls 2 inches apart onto ungreased cookie sheets.

🐦 Bake in a 350° oven for 10 to 12 minutes or till edges are firm and bottoms are lightly browned. Immediately press a chocolate kiss into the center of each cookie. Remove cookies and cool on wire racks. Makes about 54.

Nutrition information per cookie: 95 calories, 2 g protein, 11 g carbohydrate, 5 g fat (1 g saturated), 5 mg cholesterol, 25 mg sodium, 60 mg potassium.

43

To turn these into drop cookies, skip the chilling and sprinkle the dropped dough with the sugar-cinnamon mixture.

Pictured on the cover and on page 5.

Storing Cookies

🐢 To preserve the just-baked freshness of cookies, choose tightly covered containers or plastic bags. Either choice will prevent humidity from softening crisp cookies and air from drying out soft cookies. Be sure to store crisp and soft cookies separately. Most cookies can be stored successfully for up to three days at room temperature.

To freeze cookies, tightly package cookies in freezer bags or airtight containers and store for up to 12 months. Before serving, thaw for 15 minutes.

Snickerdoodles

½ cup margarine *or* butter
1½ cups all-purpose flour
1 cup sugar
1 egg
½ teaspoon vanilla
¼ teaspoon baking soda
¼ teaspoon cream of tartar
2 tablespoons sugar
1 teaspoon ground cinnamon

🐢 In a large mixing bowl beat the margarine or butter with an electric mixer on medium to high speed about 30 seconds or till softened. Add about *half* of the flour to the margarine. Then add the 1 cup sugar, egg, vanilla, baking soda, and cream of tartar. Beat till thoroughly combined, scraping the sides of the bowl occasionally. Beat in the remaining flour. Cover and chill about 1 hour or till dough is easy to handle.

🐢 In a shallow dish combine the 2 tablespoons sugar and cinnamon. Shape the dough into 1-inch balls. Roll the balls in the sugar-cinnamon mixture to coat. Place balls 2 inches apart onto ungreased cookie sheets.

🐢 Bake in a 375° oven for 10 to 11 minutes or till edges are lightly browned. Remove cookies; cool on wire racks. Makes about 36.

Nutrition information per cookie: 65 calories, 1 g protein, 10 g carbohydrate, 3 g fat (0 g saturated), 6 mg cholesterol, 37 mg sodium, 9 mg potassium.

A cookie that's so chocolaty rich it's almost like eating a brownie.

Chocolate Crinkles

   3 beaten eggs
1½ cups sugar
   4 squares (4 ounces) unsweetened
         chocolate, melted
  ½ cup cooking oil
   2 teaspoons baking powder
   2 teaspoons vanilla
   2 cups all-purpose flour
        Sifted powdered sugar

🐢 In a large mixing bowl stir together the beaten eggs, sugar, melted chocolate, cooking oil, baking powder, and vanilla. Gradually add flour to the chocolate mixture, stirring till thoroughly combined. Cover and chill for 1 to 2 hours or till the dough is easy to handle.

🐢 Shape dough into 1-inch balls. Roll the balls in powdered sugar to coat. Place balls 1 inch apart onto ungreased cookie sheets.

🐢 Bake in a 375° oven for 8 to 10 minutes or till edges are set and tops are crackled. Remove cookies and cool on wire racks. If desired, sprinkle with additional powdered sugar. Makes about 48.

Nutrition information per cookie: 79 calories, 1 g protein, 11 g carbohydrate, 4 g fat (0 g saturated), 13 mg cholesterol, 16 mg sodium, 29 mg potassium.

Show off your favorite homemade jam by spooning it into the centers of these cookies.

Jam Thumbprints

⅔ **cup margarine** *or* **butter**
1½ **cups all-purpose flour**
½ **cup sugar**
2 **egg yolks**
1 **teaspoon vanilla**
2 **slightly beaten egg whites**
1 **cup finely chopped walnuts**
⅓ **to ½ cup strawberry, cherry,** *or* **apricot jam** *or* **preserves**

🐦 In a large mixing bowl beat the margarine or butter with an electric mixer on medium to high speed about 30 seconds or till softened. Add about *half* of the flour to the margarine. Then add the sugar, egg yolks, and vanilla. Beat till thoroughly combined. Beat in the remaining flour. Cover and chill about 1 hour or till dough is easy to handle.

🐦 Shape dough into 1-inch balls. Roll balls in egg whites, then in walnuts to coat. Place balls 1 inch apart onto greased cookie sheets. Using your thumb, make an indentation in the center of each cookie.

🐦 Bake in a 375° oven for 10 to 12 minutes or till edges are lightly browned. Remove cookies and cool on wire racks.

🐦 Just before serving, fill the centers with jam or preserves. Makes about 42.

Nutrition information per cookie: 79 calories, 1 g protein, 8 g carbohydrate, 5 g fat (1 g saturated), 10 mg cholesterol, 38 mg sodium, 26 mg potassium.

Gingersnaps

2¼ **cups all-purpose flour**
 1 **cup packed brown sugar**
 ¾ **cup shortening**
 ¼ **cup molasses**
 1 **egg**
 1 **teaspoon baking soda**
 1 **teaspoon ground ginger**
 1 **teaspoon ground cinnamon**
 ½ **teaspoon ground cloves**
 ¼ **cup sugar**

✿ In a large mixing bowl place about *half* of the flour. Add the brown sugar, shortening, molasses, egg, baking soda, ginger, cinnamon, and cloves. Beat with an electric mixer on medium to high speed till thoroughly combined, scraping the sides of the bowl occasionally. Beat in the remaining flour.

✿ Shape dough into 1-inch balls. Roll the balls in sugar to coat. Place balls 2 inches apart onto ungreased cookie sheets.

✿ Bake in a 375° oven for 8 to 10 minutes or till edges are set and tops are crackled. Cool on cookie sheets for 1 minute. Remove cookies and cool on wire racks. Makes about 48.

Nutrition information per cookie: 77 calories, 1 g protein, 11 g carbohydrate, 3 g fat (1 g saturated), 4 mg cholesterol, 20 mg sodium, 40 mg potassium.

For crust, in a medium mixing bowl beat the margarine or butter and cream cheese with an electric mixer on medium to high speed about 30 seconds or till softened. Stir in the flour. Cover and chill about 1 hour or till the dough is easy to handle.

Form the chilled dough into a ball. Divide the dough into 24 equal portions. Roll each portion into a ball. Place each ball into an ungreased 1¾-inch muffin cup. Press the dough evenly against the bottom and up the sides of cup. Cover and set aside.

For filling, in a small mixing bowl beat the egg, sugar, and almond paste till almost smooth. Stir in the coarsely chopped pistachios or almonds. Fill each dough-lined muffin cup with a rounded *teaspoon* of filling.

Bake in a 325° oven for 25 to 30 minutes or till tops are lightly browned. Cool slightly in pans. Remove tarts from pans and cool on wire racks.

Store, tightly covered, at room temperature for up to 1 week. Or, freeze in a moisture and vaporproof freezer container for up to 12 months.

To serve, if frozen, cover tarts and thaw at room temperature. If desired, pipe or swirl Chocolate Decorating Frosting on top of each, then top with a pistachio nut or almond. Makes 24.

*K*eep a bowl of pistachios by your TV chair and shell a supply for these cookies while you watch your favorite shows.

*P*istachio-Almond Tarts

½ cup margarine *or* butter
1 3-ounce package cream cheese
1 cup all-purpose flour
1 egg
½ cup sugar
½ of an 8-ounce can (½ cup) almond paste, crumbled
¼ cup coarsely chopped pistachio nuts *or* almonds
Chocolate Decorating Frosting (optional)
Pistachio nuts *or* almonds (optional)

Chocolate Decorating Frosting: In a small mixing bowl beat 3 tablespoons *shortening* and ½ teaspoon *vanilla* with an electric mixer on medium speed for 30 seconds. Add ½ cup sifted *powdered sugar* and 3 tablespoons *unsweetened cocoa powder.* Beat well. Add 2 teaspoons *milk.* Gradually beat in an additional ½ cup sifted *powdered sugar* and enough additional *milk* to make of piping consistency.

Nutrition information per tart: 111 calories, 2 g protein, 10 g carbohydrate, 7 g fat (2 g saturated), 13 mg cholesterol, 58 mg sodium, 57 mg potassium.

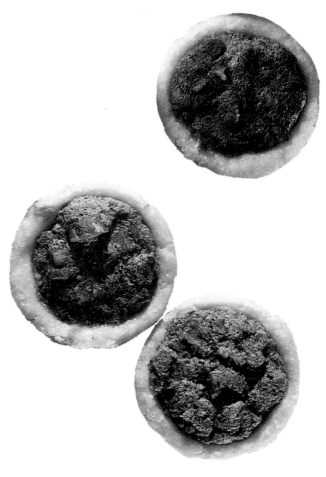

The full flavor of pecan pie is packed into each bite-size tea cake.

Pecan Tea Cakes

½ **cup margarine** *or* **butter**
1 **3-ounce package cream cheese**
1 **cup all-purpose flour**
1 **beaten egg**
¾ **cup packed brown sugar**
1 **tablespoon margarine** *or* **butter, melted**
1 **teaspoon vanilla**
½ **teaspoon almond extract**
1 **cup chopped pecans**

🌰 For crust, in a small mixing bowl beat the ½ cup margarine or butter and cream cheese with an electric mixer on medium speed about 30 seconds or till softened. Stir in the flour. Cover and chill about 1 hour or till dough is easy to handle.

🌰 Form the chilled dough into a ball. Divide the dough into 24 equal portions. Roll each portion into a ball. Place each ball into an ungreased 1¾-inch muffin cup. Press the dough evenly against the bottom and up the sides of cup. Cover and set aside.

🌰 For filling, in a small mixing bowl stir together the egg, brown sugar, melted margarine or butter, vanilla, almond extract, and pecans. Fill each dough-lined muffin cup with a scant *tablespoon* of filling.

🌰 Bake in a 375° oven for 15 to 18 minutes or till filling is set and crust is lightly browned. Cool slightly in pans. Remove tea cakes from pans and cool on wire racks. Makes 24.

Nutrition information per tea cake: 128 calories, 1 g protein, 11 g carbohydrate, 9 g fat (2 g saturated), 13 mg cholesterol, 65 mg sodium, 55 mg potassium.

49

If you'd rather, sprinkle the tarts with powdered sugar and omit the jelly.

Mini Chess Tarts

1   11-ounce package piecrust mix
½   cup plain yogurt
2   slightly beaten eggs
¾   cup sugar
3   tablespoons margarine *or* butter, melted
2   tablespoons milk
1½ teaspoons cornmeal
½   teaspoon finely shredded lemon peel
1½ teaspoons lemon juice
    Jelly (optional)

🍂 For crust, in a medium mixing bowl stir together the piecrust mix and yogurt till moistened. Form the dough into a ball. Divide the dough into 36 equal portions. Roll each portion into a ball. Place each ball into an ungreased 1¾-inch muffin cup. Press the dough evenly against the bottom and up the sides of cup. Cover and set aside.

🍂 For filling, in a small mixing bowl stir together the eggs, sugar, margarine or butter, milk, cornmeal, lemon peel, and lemon juice. Fill each dough-lined muffin cup with about *2 teaspoons* of filling.

🍂 Bake in a 350° oven for 25 to 30 minutes or till lightly browned and set in centers. Cool slightly in pans. Remove tarts from pans and cool on wire racks.

🍂 To serve, if desired, spoon *½ teaspoon* jelly into the center of each tart. Makes 36.

Nutrition information per tart: 92 calories,
1 g protein, 11 g carbohydrate, 5 g fat (1 g saturated),
12 mg cholesterol, 80 mg sodium, 22 mg potassium.

Gramma Carey's Tea Tarts

⅓   cup margarine *or* butter
1   3-ounce package cream cheese, softened
1   cup all-purpose flour
2   tablespoons sugar
¼   cup fruit preserves
½   cup semisweet chocolate pieces
1   tablespoon shortening

🍂 In a medium mixing bowl beat the margarine or butter and cream cheese with an electric mixer on medium to high speed about 30 seconds or till softened. Add the flour and sugar. Beat till well mixed. Divide the dough in half. Form *each* half into a ball.

🍂 On a lightly floured surface, roll *each* half into a 10x7½-inch rectangle. Cut the rectangle into 2½-inch squares. Spoon about *½ teaspoon* preserves onto center of *each* square. Moisten edges of each pastry square with water. Fold dough over filling to form triangles. With a fork, crimp edges together to seal. Place the triangles onto ungreased cookie sheets.

🍂 Bake in a 425° oven for 8 to 10 minutes or till lightly browned. Remove tarts and cool on wire racks.

🍂 Meanwhile, in a small heavy saucepan melt the chocolate pieces and shortening over low heat, stirring occasionally. Dip one tip of each triangle in the chocolate mixture. Place tarts on waxed paper till chocolate sets. Makes 24.

Nutrition information per tart: 86 calories,
1 g protein, 9 g carbohydrate, 5 g fat (1 g saturated),
4 mg cholesterol, 40 mg sodium, 25 mg potassium.

These tender, cakey cookies are the perfect treat to serve along with an afternoon cup of tea.

Spiced Chocolate Tea Cakes

1½ **cups all-purpose flour**
¼ **cup unsweetened cocoa powder**
¼ **teaspoon ground nutmeg** *or* **ground cardamom**
¼ **teaspoon baking powder**
½ **cup margarine** *or* **butter**
¾ **cup sugar**
1 **egg yolk**
⅓ **cup milk**
   Sifted powdered sugar

🍂 In a small mixing bowl stir together the flour, cocoa powder, nutmeg or cardamom, and baking powder. Set aside.

🍂 In a large mixing bowl beat the margarine or butter and sugar with an electric mixer on medium speed about 30 seconds or till fluffy. Beat in the egg yolk. Add about *half* of the flour mixture. Then add the milk and beat till well blended. Beat or stir in the remaining flour mixture. (If dough is too stiff to pipe, stir in additional milk as necessary.)

🍂 Spoon dough into a decorating bag fitted with a large star tip (½-inch opening). On greased cookie sheets pipe dough into 1½-inch shells, pulling the pastry bag toward you as you pipe.

🍂 Bake in a 350° oven for 12 to 14 minutes or till set. Cool on cookie sheets for 1 minute. Remove cookies and cool on wire racks. Sift powdered sugar over tops. Makes about 30.

Nutrition information tea cake: 76 calories, 1 g protein, 10 g carbohydrate, 3 g fat (1 g saturated), 7 mg cholesterol, 40 mg sodium, 13 mg potassium.

No cookie press? These buttery morsels are just as delicious dropped by the teaspoonful on a cookie sheet.

Spritz

1½   **cups margarine *or* butter**
3½   **cups all-purpose flour**
  1   **cup sugar**
  1   **egg**
  1   **teaspoon baking powder**
  1   **teaspoon vanilla**
  ½   **teaspoon almond extract (optional)**
       Desired small multicolored decorative candies, finely chopped dried fruits *or* nuts, *or* colored sugars (optional)

🐢 In a large mixing bowl beat the margarine or butter with an electric mixer on medium to high speed about 30 seconds or till softened. Add *1 cup* of the flour. Then add the sugar, egg, baking powder, vanilla, and, if desired, almond extract. Beat till thoroughly combined. Beat in the remaining flour. *Do not chill dough.*

🐢 Pack the dough into a cookie press. Force dough through press onto ungreased cookie sheets. If desired, decorate with decorative candies, fruits, nuts, or colored sugars.

🐢 Bake in a 375° oven for 8 to 10 minutes or till edges of cookies are firm but not brown. Remove cookies and cool on wire racks. Makes about 84.

Nutrition information per cookie: 56 calories, 1 g protein, 6 g carbohydrate, 3 g fat (1 g saturated), 3 mg cholesterol, 42 mg sodium, 8 mg potassium.

Whole Wheat Spritz: Prepare Spritz as directed at left, *except* reduce all-purpose flour to *2½ cups* and add 1 cup *whole wheat flour.*

Nutrition information per cookie: 56 calories, 1 g protein, 6 g carbohydrate, 3 g fat (1 g saturated), 3 mg cholesterol, 42 mg sodium, 12 mg potassium.

Nutty Spritz: Prepare Spritz as directed at left, *except* reduce all-purpose flour to *3 cups* and add 1 cup finely ground *almonds or pecans.*

Nutrition information per cookie: 59 calories, 1 g protein, 6 g carbohydrate, 4 g fat (1 g saturated), 3 mg cholesterol, 42 mg sodium, 14 mg potassium.

Chocolate Spritz: Prepare Spritz as directed at left, *except* reduce all-purpose flour to *3¼ cups.* Add ¼ cup *unsweetened cocoa powder* with the sugar.

Nutrition information per cookie: 56 calories, 1 g protein, 6 g carbohydrate, 3 g fat (1 g saturated), 3 mg cholesterol, 42 mg sodium, 7 mg potassium.

Boo! What's more fun at Halloween than carving and lighting a pumpkin so ol' Jack glows? Making scary faces in cookies, and eating them, too!

Spooky Cookies

1¾ **cups whole wheat flour**
1 **cup all-purpose flour**
1 **teaspoon pumpkin pie spice**
½ **teaspoon baking soda**
¼ **teaspoon salt**
½ **cup margarine** *or* **butter**
1 **cup packed brown sugar**
1 **egg**
½ **teaspoon vanilla**
½ **cup dairy sour cream**
3 **ounces yellow** *or* **red clear hard candy, finely crushed**

🐾 In a medium mixing bowl stir together the whole wheat flour, all-purpose flour, pumpkin pie spice, baking soda, and salt. Set aside.

🐾 In a large mixing bowl beat the margarine or butter with an electric mixer on medium to high speed about 30 seconds or till softened. Add the brown sugar and beat till fluffy. Add egg and vanilla. Beat till thoroughly combined, scraping the sides of the bowl occasionally. Alternately add the flour mixture and sour cream, beating well after each addition.

🐾 Divide the dough in half. Cover and chill about 3 hours or till dough is easy to handle.

🐾 On a lightly floured surface, roll *each* half of the dough to ⅛-inch thickness. Using a 6-inch pumpkin-shape cutter or a knife, cut dough into pumpkin shapes. Place onto foil-lined cookie sheets. Using hors d'oeuvre cutters or a sharp knife, cut out eyes, mouths, or noses. Use dough scraps to make noses or eyebrows to attach. With a knife, make the stem and vein marks in cookies. Spoon enough candy into each cutout to fill hole.

🐾 Bake in a 350° oven for 6 to 8 minutes or till edges are very lightly browned. Cool on cookie sheets for 10 minutes. Peel off foil. Cool cookies on wire racks. Store in an airtight container. Makes about 10 large cookies.

Nutrition information per cookie: 343 calories, 5 g protein, 54 g carbohydrate, 13 g fat (3 g saturated), 26 mg cholesterol, 224 mg sodium, 202 mg potassium.

Use the tip of a table knife to score veins in the leaves.

Maple Leaves

1 cup margarine *or* butter
⅔ cup packed brown sugar
½ cup pure maple syrup *or* maple-flavored syrup
⅓ cup milk
3½ cups all-purpose flour
½ teaspoon baking soda
½ teaspoon ground ginger

🍂 In a medium saucepan combine the margarine or butter, brown sugar, and maple or maple-flavored syrup. Bring the mixture to boiling, stirring occasionally. Remove from heat. Cool to room temperature. Stir in the milk.

🍂 In a large mixing bowl stir together the flour, baking soda, and ginger. Add the cooled syrup mixture to the flour mixture. Stir till thoroughly combined. Divide the dough in half. Cover and chill about 3 hours or till the dough is easy to handle.

🍂 On a lightly floured surface, roll *each* half of dough to ⅛- to ¼-inch thickness. Using a maple- or other leaf-shape cutter, cut dough into leaf shapes. Place 1-inch apart onto ungreased cookie sheets. Using a table knife, score vein designs in the cookies.

🍂 Bake in a 375° oven for 6 to 8 minutes or till bottoms are lightly browned. Remove cookies; cool on wire racks. Makes about 42.

Nutrition information per cookie: 98 calories, 1 g protein, 14 g carbohydrate, 4 g fat (1 g saturated), 0 mg cholesterol, 67 mg sodium, 29 mg potassium.

Brown Sugar Cutouts

⅓ cup shortening
⅓ cup margarine *or* butter
1 teaspoon instant-coffee crystals
1¾ cups all-purpose flour
¼ cup whole wheat flour
¾ cup packed brown sugar
1 egg
1 teaspoon baking powder
½ teaspoon ground cinnamon
½ teaspoon vanilla
Creamy Frosting

🍂 In a mixing bowl beat shortening and margarine with an electric mixer on medium to high speed for 30 seconds. Dissolve coffee crystals in 1 tablespoon warm *water*. Add to margarine mixture along with *¾ cup* all-purpose flour. Then add whole wheat flour, brown sugar, egg, baking powder, cinnamon, vanilla, and ¼ teaspoon *salt*; beat well. Beat in remaining flour. Divide dough in half. Cover; chill about 3 hours or till easy to handle.

🍂 On a lightly floured surface, roll *each* half of the dough to ⅛-inch thickness. Using 2- to 2½-inch cutters, cut dough into desired shapes. Place 1 inch apart onto ungreased cookie sheets.

🍂 Bake in 375° oven for 7 to 8 minutes or till edges are firm. Cool on cookie sheet for 1 minute. Remove cookies; cool on wire racks. Frost with Creamy Frosting. Makes about 40.

Creamy Frosting: Beat 3 tablespoons *margarine or butter* about 30 seconds or till softened. Gradually add 1 cup sifted *powdered sugar*, beating well. Beat in 2 tablespoons *milk* and ¼ teaspoon *vanilla*. Slowly beat in an additional 1¼ cups sifted *powdered sugar* and enough *milk*, if necessary, to make of spreading consistency.

Nutrition information per cookie: 97 calories, 1 g protein, 14 g carbohydrate, 4 g fat (1 g saturated), 5 mg cholesterol, 38 mg sodium, 29 mg potassium.

If you wish, dress up these cookies by stirring 2 tablespoons small multicolored decorative candies into the dough with the remaining flour.

Pictured on the cover.

Sugar Cookie Cutouts

⅓ **cup shortening**
⅓ **cup margarine *or* butter**
2 **cups all-purpose flour**
¾ **cup sugar**
1 **egg**
1 **tablespoon milk**
1 **teaspoon baking powder**
1 **teaspoon vanilla**
   Dash salt
   Powdered Sugar Icing (optional)

🐢 In a large mixing bowl beat the shortening and margarine or butter with an electric mixer on medium to high speed about 30 seconds or till softened. Add about *half* of the flour. Then add the sugar, egg, milk, baking powder, vanilla, and salt. Beat till thoroughly combined, scraping the sides of bowl occasionally. Beat or stir in the remaining flour. Divide dough in half. Cover and chill about 3 hours or till dough is easy to handle.

🐢 On a lightly floured surface, roll *each* half of the dough to ⅛-inch thickness. Using 2½-inch cutters, cut dough into desired shapes. Place 1-inch apart onto ungreased cookie sheets.

🐢 Bake in a 375° oven for 7 to 8 minutes or till the bottoms are very lightly browned. Cool on cookie sheets for 1 minute. Remove cookies and cool on wire racks. If desired, decorate cookies with Powdered Sugar Icing. Makes about 42.

Powdered Sugar Icing: In a small mixing bowl stir together 1 cup sifted *powdered sugar,* ¼ teaspoon *vanilla,* and enough *milk* (about 1 tablespoon) to make of drizzling or piping consistency. If desired, color with food coloring.

Nutrition information per cookie: 62 calories, 1 g protein, 8 g carbohydrate, 3 g fat (1 g saturated), 5 mg cholesterol, 28 mg sodium, 9 mg potassium.

To change the shape, all you have to do is change the cutter.

Chocolate-Pistachio Hearts

    1 cup magarine *or* butter
    ⅔ cup packed brown sugar
    1 teaspoon vanilla
    1 beaten egg
 2¼ cups all-purpose flour
    ¼ cup unsweetened cocoa powder
    ¾ cup finely chopped pistachio nuts
    ¾ cup semisweet chocolate pieces
    1 tablespoon shortening
    ¼ cup ground pistachio nuts

🌰 In a medium saucepan combine the margarine or butter and brown sugar. Cook and stir over medium heat till margarine is melted. Remove from heat. Stir in the vanilla. Cool for 15 minutes.

🌰 Stir the beaten egg, flour, and cocoa powder into the margarine mixture till combined. Stir in the ¾ cup pistachio nuts. Divide dough in half. Cover and chill about 30 minutes or till dough is easy to handle.

🌰 On a lightly floured surface, roll *each* half of dough to ¼-inch thickness. Using a 2-inch heart-shape cutter, cut dough into heart shapes. Place 1-inch apart onto ungreased cookie sheets.

🌰 Bake in a 350° oven about 9 minutes or till firm. Remove cookies and cool on wire racks.

🌰 In a small heavy saucepan melt the chocolate pieces and shortening over low heat, stirring occasionally. Dip half of each heart into the chocolate mixture. Dip the chocolate-covered edges into the ground pistachio nuts. Place cookies on a wire rack till chocolate is set. Makes about 48.

Nutrition information per cookie: 98 calories, 1 g protein, 10 g carbohydrate, 6 g fat (1 g saturated), 4 mg cholesterol, 47 mg sodium, 51 mg potassium.

Old World Cookie Treasures

Rejoice in these treasured ethnic recipes, brought here by families from all over the world and shared with love. German, Italian, and Scandinavian cookies, as well as others in this collection, have been adapted to our country, for our times.

Almond Biscotti
(see recipe, page 64)

Eggnog Kringla
(see recipe, page 69)

For Valentine's Day cookies, use heart-shape cookie cutters and tint the icing a cotton-candy shade of pink.

Zimtstern

  2 **egg whites**
1½ **cups almonds, toasted and ground**
  ¾ **cup hazelnuts (filberts), toasted and ground**
  2 **tablespoons all-purpose flour**
  1 **teaspoon ground cinnamon**
  ¼ **teaspoon ground nutmeg**
  1 **cup sugar**
      Powdered sugar
1½ **cups sifted powdered sugar**
      Milk
      Several drops food coloring

🐦 In a large mixing bowl let egg whites stand at room temperature for 30 minutes. Meanwhile, line 2 large cookie sheets with parchment paper. In a medium mixing bowl mix almonds, hazelnuts, flour, cinnamon, and nutmeg. Set aside.

🐦 Beat egg whites with an electric mixer on medium speed till soft peaks form (tips curl). Gradually add sugar, *1 tablespoon* at a time, beating on high speed till stiff peaks form (tips stand straight) and sugar is *almost* dissolved. Fold nut mixture into egg whites. Cover and let stand for 30 minutes.

🐦 Sprinkle some powdered sugar lightly over a surface. Roll dough on surface to ¼-inch thickness. Using a floured 2- to 2½-inch star-shape cutter, cut dough into stars. Place 1 inch apart onto prepared cookie sheets.

🐦 Bake in a 325° oven about 10 minutes or till lightly browned and crisp. Remove cookies and cool on wire racks.

🐦 Meanwhile, for frosting, in a small bowl stir together 1½ cups powdered sugar and enough milk (1 to 2 tablespoons) to make of thin spreading consistency. Tint with food coloring. Spread on cookies. Makes about 32.

Nutrition information per cookie: 99 calories, 2 g protein, 13 g carbohydrate, 5 g fat (0 g saturated), 0 mg cholesterol, 5 mg sodium, 61 mg potassium.

Walnuts in disguise! The bubbly, crispy coating on the walnuts comes from brushing them with the egg white and sugar mixture.

Chocolate-Nut Cookies

½ **cup shortening**
3 **beaten eggs**
1½ **cups sugar**
4 **squares (4 ounces) unsweetened chocolate, melted and cooled**
2 **teaspoons baking powder**
2 **teaspoons vanilla**
2 **cups all-purpose flour**
⅓ **cup sugar**
1 **beaten egg white**
About 60 walnut halves

🐦 In a large mixing bowl beat the shortening with an electric mixer on medium to high speed about 30 seconds or till softened. Add the eggs, 1½ cups sugar, melted and cooled chocolate, baking powder, and vanilla. Beat till well combined, scraping the sides of the bowl. Gradually stir in the flour till thoroughly combined. Cover and chill for 1 to 2 hours or till dough is easy to handle.

🐦 Meanwhile, stir together ⅓ cup sugar and beaten egg white. Place walnut halves on waxed paper; brush with egg white and sugar mixture. Set aside.

🐦 Shape dough into 1-inch balls. Place 2 inches apart onto ungreased cookie sheets. Place a walnut half in the center of *each* ball, pressing lightly.

🐦 Bake in a 375° oven for 8 to 10 minutes or till edges are set. Remove cookies and cool on wire racks. Makes about 60.

Nutrition information per cookie: 91 calories, 2 g protein, 10 g carbohydrate, 5 g fat (1 g saturated), 11 mg cholesterol, 14 mg sodium, 44 mg potassium.

Be careful, these crunchy little cookies are addictive.

Pfeffernuesse

⅓ **cup molasses**
¼ **cup margarine** *or* **butter**
2 **cups all-purpose flour**
¼ **cup packed brown sugar**
¾ **teaspoon ground cinnamon**
½ **teaspoon baking soda**
¼ **teaspoon ground cardamom**
¼ **teaspoon ground allspice**
⅛ **teaspoon pepper**
1 **beaten egg**

🐦 In a large saucepan combine the molasses and margarine or butter. Heat and stir over low heat till margarine melts. Remove from heat. Cool to room temperature.

🐦 In a large mixing bowl stir together the flour, brown sugar, cinnamon, baking soda, cardamom, allspice, and pepper. Set aside.

🐦 Stir the egg into the molasses mixture. Gradually stir in flour mixture. Transfer the dough to a bowl. Cover and chill about 1 hour or till dough is easy to handle.

🐦 Divide dough into 12 portions. On a lightly floured surface, roll *each* portion into a 10-inch rope. Cut ropes into ½-inch pieces. Place pieces ½ inch apart onto ungreased shallow baking pans.

🐦 Bake in a 350° oven for 10 to 12 minutes or till edges are firm and bottoms are lightly browned. Remove cookies and cool on paper towels. Makes about 240.

Nutrition information per cookie: 8 calories, 0 g protein, 1 g carbohydrate, 0 g fat (0 g saturated), 1 mg cholesterol, 4 mg sodium, 8 mg potassium.

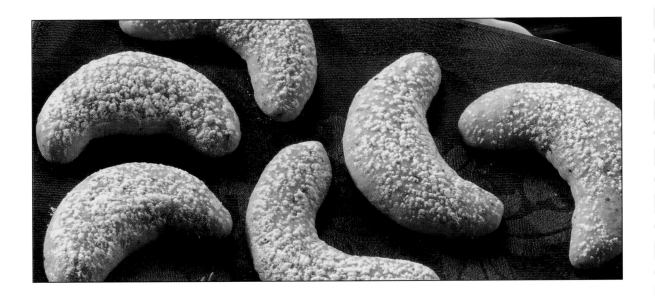

For a spectacular gift to give a friend, package these nutty German cookies in a fancy tin and present them with a bag of hazelnut-flavored coffee.

Hazelnut Crescents

1 **cup margarine** *or* **butter**
½ **cup sugar**
1 **teaspoon vanilla**
2 **cups all-purpose flour**
½ **cup ground hazelnuts (filberts)**
   Sifted powdered sugar

In a large mixing bowl beat the margarine or butter, sugar, and vanilla with an electric mixer on medium speed till light and fluffy. Add the flour and nuts. Beat till well combined.

Using about *2 teaspoons* of dough for *each* cookie, shape into crescents, tapering ends. Place crescents 1 inch apart onto ungreased cookie sheets.

Bake in a 325° oven for 12 to 15 minutes or till bottoms of crescents are lightly browned. Remove cookies and cool on wire racks. Sprinkle with powdered sugar. Makes about 60.

Nutrition information per cookie: 55 calories, 1 g protein, 5 g carbohydrate, 4 g fat (1 g saturated), 0 mg cholesterol, 36 mg sodium, 10 mg potassium.

Be sure to make some of these German spice cookies in the shape of pigs—they're said to bring good luck.

Ginger Cutouts

½ **cup shortening**
2½ **cups all-purpose flour**
½ **cup sugar**
½ **cup molasses**
1 **egg**
1 **teaspoon baking soda**
1 **teaspoon ground ginger**
½ **teaspoon ground cinnamon**
½ **teaspoon ground cloves**
   Powdered Sugar Icing
   Candied fruit
   Whole *or* sliced blanched almonds

🐷 In a large mixing bowl beat shortening with an electric mixer on medium to high speed about 30 seconds or till softened. Add about *half* of the flour to the shortening. Then add the sugar, molasses, egg, baking soda, ginger, cinnamon, and cloves. Beat till thoroughly combined. Then beat or stir in the remaining flour. Divide dough in half.

Cover dough and chill about 3 hours or till easy to handle.

🐷 On a lightly floured surface, roll *each* half of the dough to ⅛- to ¼-inch thickness. Using 2- to 2½-inch cookie cutters, cut dough into desired shapes. Place 1 inch apart onto greased cookie sheets.

🐷 Bake in a 375° oven for 5 to 6 minutes or till edges are firm. Cool on the cookie sheets for 1 minute. Remove cookies and cool on wire racks. Decorate as desired with Powdered Sugar Icing, candied fruit, and almonds. Makes about 36.

Powdered Sugar Icing: In a small bowl stir together 1 cup sifted *powdered sugar,* ¼ teaspoon *vanilla,* and enough *milk* (about 1 tablespoon) to make of spreading consistency.

Nutrition information per cookie: 103 calories, 1 g protein, 16 g carbohydrate, 4 g fat (1 g saturated), 6 mg cholesterol, 26 mg sodium, 64 mg potassium.

When it comes to German cookies, nuts and chocolate are two of the favorite and most commonly used ingredients.

Nut Meringues

2 **egg whites**
½ **teaspoon vanilla**
⅔ **cup sugar**
1 **cup very finely chopped almonds**
   and/or **hazelnuts (filberts)**
½ **cup semisweet chocolate pieces**
1 **teaspoon shortening**

 In a medium mixing bowl let egg whites stand at room temperature for 30 minutes. Meanwhile, line 2 cookie sheets with parchment paper. Set aside.

 Add vanilla to egg whites. Beat with an electric mixer on medium speed till soft peaks form (tips curl). Gradually add sugar, *1 tablespoon* at a time, beating on high speed till stiff peaks form (tips stand straight) and sugar is *almost* dissolved. Fold in nuts.

 Drop mixture by slightly rounded teaspoons, 2 inches apart, onto prepared cookie sheets.

 Bake in a 325° oven for 15 to 20 minutes or till edges are lightly browned. Remove cookies and cool on wire racks.

 In a small heavy saucepan melt the chocolate and shortening over low heat, stirring occasionally. Drizzle over cookies. Makes about 30.

Nutrition information per cookie: 49 calories, 1 g protein, 5 g carbohydrate, 3 g fat (0 g saturated), 0 mg cholesterol, 4 mg sodium, 44 mg potassium.

*D*unk this crunchy cookie
in a steaming cup of coffee.

Pictured on the cover and
on page 57.

*A*lmond Biscotti

⅓ **cup margarine** *or* **butter**
2 **cups all-purpose flour**
⅔ **cup sugar**
2 **eggs**
2 **teaspoons baking powder**
1 **teaspoon vanilla**
1½ **cups slivered almonds** *or* **hazelnuts,**
    (filberts), finely chopped
1 **beaten egg yolk**
1 **tablespoon milk** *or* **water**
1 **cup milk chocolate** *or* **semisweet**
    chocolate pieces
2 **tablespoons shortening**

🍂 In a large mixing bowl beat the margarine
or butter with an electric mixer on medium to
high speed about 30 seconds or till softened.
Add about *half* of the flour to the margarine.
Then add the sugar, whole eggs, baking
powder, and vanilla. Beat till thoroughly
combined, scraping the sides of the bowl
occasionally. Then beat or stir in the remaining
flour and almonds or hazelnuts. Divide dough
in half.

🍂 Shape each portion into a 9x2x1½-inch
loaf. Place the loaves about 4 inches apart on a
lightly greased cookie sheet. Stir together the
egg yolk and milk or water. Brush mixture over
loaves.

🍂 Bake in a 375° oven for 25 minutes. Cool
on the cookie sheet for 30 minutes.

🍂 Cut each loaf diagonally into ½-inch-thick
slices. Lay slices, cut side down, on an
ungreased cookie sheet. Bake in a 325° oven
for 8 minutes. Turn slices over. Bake for 8 to
10 minutes more or till dry and crisp. Remove
cookies and cool on wire racks.

🍂 In a small heavy saucepan melt chocolate
pieces and shortening over low heat, stirring
occasionally. Place cooled cookies, flat side up,
on waxed paper. With a spoon, drizzle
chocolate atop cookies or dip cookies into
melted chocolate. For a design on the dipped
cookies, run a fork or the tip of a knife through
the chocolate while still soft. Let chocolate set
up before serving. Makes about 30.

Nutrition information per cookie: 144 calories,
3 g protein, 15 g carbohydrate, 8 g fat (1 g saturated),
22 mg cholesterol, 53 mg sodium, 81 mg potassium.

🍂 In a small mixing bowl stir together the flour, baking powder, nutmeg, and cardamom. Set aside.

🍂 In a large mixing bowl beat the eggs with an electric mixer on high speed about 4 minutes or till thick and lemon colored. With the mixer on medium speed, gradually beat in the sugar. Then beat in the melted margarine or butter and the vanilla. Add the flour mixture. Beat on low speed till combined, scraping the sides of bowl occasionally.

🍂 Heat an electric pizzelle iron according to the manufacturer's directions. (Or, heat a nonelectric pizzelle iron on the range-top over medium heat till a drop of water sizzles on the grid. Reduce heat to medium-low.)

🍂 Place a slightly rounded tablespoon of batter slightly off center toward back of grid. Close lid. Bake according to manufacturer's directions. (For a nonelectric iron, bake for 30 to 60 seconds or till golden, turning once.) Turn wafer out onto a paper towel to cool. Repeat with remaining batter. Makes about 18.

Nutrition information per cookie: 122 calories, 22 g protein, 18 g carbohydrate, 4 g fat (1 g saturated), 36 mg cholesterol, 98 mg sodium, 27 mg potassium.

Italian pizzelles, like their cousins, French gaufrettes and Norwegian krumkake, are baked in an easy-to-use iron.

To divide the pizzelles into smaller pieces, cut them while they're still hot. This way, the pieces will have clean-cut edges.

Pizzelles

2 **cups all-purpose flour**
1 **tablespoon baking powder**
1½ **teaspoons ground nutmeg**
½ **teaspoon ground cardamom**
3 **eggs**
¾ **cup sugar**
⅓ **cup margarine** *or* **butter, melted**
2 **teaspoons vanilla**

You'll find many of the flavors typical of Greek desserts packed into these small cookies—honey, orange, spices, and nuts.

Pictured on the cover.

Greek Honey-Walnut Balls

⅓ **cup honey**
¼ **cup sugar**
½ **teaspoon finely shredded orange peel (set aside)**
¼ **cup orange juice**
2 **inches stick cinnamon**
3 **whole cloves**
1 **cup ground walnuts**
1 **cup margarine *or* butter**
3 **cups all-purpose flour**
½ **cup sugar**
¼ **cup orange juice**
2 **tablespoons brandy**
¾ **teaspoon baking powder**
½ **teaspoon ground cinnamon**
¼ **teaspoon baking soda**
¼ **teaspoon ground cloves**
¼ **teaspoon ground nutmeg**
½ **cup finely chopped walnuts**

🍂 In a small saucepan combine the honey, ¼ cup sugar, ¼ cup orange juice, stick cinnamon, and whole cloves. Bring to boiling; reduce heat. Boil gently, uncovered, for 5 minutes. Strain syrup, discarding spices. Remove ¼ cup of the syrup. Set remaining syrup aside.

🍂 In a medium bowl combine the ground walnuts and the orange peel. Stir in the ¼ cup syrup; set aside.

🍂 For dough, in a large mixing bowl beat the margarine or butter with an electric mixer on medium to high speed about 30 seconds or till softened. Add about *half* of the flour to the margarine. Then add the ½ cup sugar, ¼ cup orange juice, brandy, baking powder, ground cinnamon, baking soda, ground cloves, and nutmeg. Beat till well combined. Then beat or stir in the remaining flour.

🍂 Shape dough into 1¼-inch balls. Using your finger, press a hole in the center of each ball of dough. Place about ½ *teaspoon* of the nut mixture in the center of *each* ball. Bring dough up around mixture, enclosing it completely. Place balls, seam side down, about 2 inches apart onto greased cookie sheets. With a knife, score a crisscross, forming an X, on the top of each ball.

🍂 Bake in a 350° oven for 18 to 20 minutes or till set. Cool on cookie sheets for 1 minute.

🍂 Meanwhile, warm reserved syrup over low heat; do not boil. Brush tops of hot cookies with warm syrup or dip tops into syrup. Sprinkle with finely chopped nuts. Cool on wire racks. Makes about 40.

Nutrition information per cookie: 120 calories, 2 g protein, 13 g carbohydrate, 7 g fat (1 g saturated), 0 mg cholesterol, 65 mg sodium, 37 mg potassium.

Traditionally, Sand Tarts, also known as Norwegian sandbakkelse, are molded in tiny tart pans. We found that by rolling out the dough and cutting it into shapes, you can create the same rich and delicate cookies and have a pretty presentation as well.

Sand Tarts

1	cup margarine *or* butter
2½	cups all-purpose flour
2	cups sugar
2	eggs
½	teaspoon lemon extract
1	beaten egg white
¼	cup sugar
½	teaspoon ground cinnamon
	Sliced almonds

🍂 In a large mixing bowl beat the margarine or butter with an electric mixer on medium to high speed about 30 seconds or till softened. Add about *half* of the flour to the margarine. Then add the 2 cups sugar, eggs, and lemon extract. Beat till mixture is thoroughly combined, scraping the sides of the bowl occasionally. Then beat or stir in the remaining flour.

🍂 Divide dough in half. Cover and chill about 3 hours or till dough is easy to handle.

🍂 On a lightly floured surface, roll *each* portion of dough to ⅛-inch thickness. Using 2- or 2½-inch cookie cutters, cut into desired shapes. Place cookies about 1 inch apart onto greased cookie sheets. Brush tops of cookies with beaten egg white. Combine the ¼ cup sugar and cinnamon. Sprinkle mixture over cookies. Arrange 3 or 5 almond slices on each cookie.

🍂 Bake in a 375° oven for 8 to 9 minutes or till edges are lightly browned. Remove cookies and cool on wire racks. Makes about 70.

Nutrition information per cookie: 69 calories, 1 g protein, 10g carbohydrate, 3 g fat (1 g saturated), 6 mg cholesterol, 33 mg sodium, 15 mg potassium.

A rosette iron gives these crisp Scandinavian delicacies their whimsical shape.

Rosettes

1   **egg**
1   **tablespoon sugar**
½   **cup all-purpose flour**
½   **cup milk**
1   **teaspoon vanilla**
     Shortening *or* **cooking oil for deep-fat frying**
     Powdered sugar

🌰 In a medium mixing bowl stir together the egg and sugar. Add the flour, milk, and vanilla. Beat with a rotary beater till smooth.

🌰 Heat a rosette iron in deep hot fat (375°) for 30 seconds. Remove iron from fat and drain on paper towels.

🌰 Dip the hot iron into batter (batter should extend three-fourths of the way up the side of iron). Immediately dip iron into hot fat. Fry for 15 to 20 seconds or till golden. Lift iron out of fat, tipping slightly to drain.

🌰 Push rosette off iron with fork onto wire racks lined with paper towels. Repeat with remaining batter, reheating iron about 10 seconds each time.

🌰 Cool rosettes and sift powdered sugar over them. Makes about 25.

Nutrition information per cookie: 40 calories, 1 g protein, 3 g carbohydrate, 3 g fat (0 g saturated), 11 mg cholesterol, 6 mg sodium, 16 mg potassium.

The shape of these soft, cakelike cookies is a simplified kringla shape. The traditional kringla looks like a pretzel. If you prefer the traditional shape, roll rounded tablespoonfuls of dough into 10-inch ropes. Shape each into a loop, crossing 1½ inches from ends. Twist rope at crossing point. Then lift loop over to ends and seal, forming a pretzel shape.

Pictured on the cover and on page 57.

*E*ggnog Kringla

    4 cups all-purpose flour
    1 teaspoon baking powder
   ½ teaspoon baking soda
   ½ teaspoon ground nutmeg
   ¾ cup butter *(not margarine)*
1½ cups sugar
    1 egg
    1 cup dairy *or* **nondairy eggnog**
       Sifted powdered sugar (optional)
       Gound nutmeg (optional)

🐦 In a large bowl stir together flour, baking powder, baking soda, and nutmeg. Set aside.

🐦 In a large mixing bowl beat the butter with an electric mixer on medium to high speed about 30 seconds or till softened. Add the sugar and beat till fluffy. Add egg and beat well. Add the flour mixture and eggnog alternately to the margarine mixture, beating till well mixed. (If the dough gets too stiff for your mixer as you're adding the flour mixture, stir in the last part by hand.) Cover; chill at least 4 hours (dough may be slightly sticky).

🐦 Working with *half* of the dough at a time, on a floured surface, roll *rounded tablespoonfuls* of the dough into pencillike strips, about 8 inches long and ½ inch thick. (Keep remaining dough chilled.) On an ungreased cookie sheet loop one end of the strip over the other end to form an oval with the two ends overlapping.

🐦 Bake in a 350° oven for 6 to 8 minutes or till edges are just lightly browned. Remove cookies and cool on wire racks. If desired, sprinkle with powdered sugar and nutmeg. Makes about 60 cookies.

Nutrition information per cookie: 73 calories, 1 g protein, 11 g carbohydrate, 3 g fat (1 g saturated), 10 mg cholesterol, 39 mg sodium, 11 mg potassium.

The perfect cookie to serve with tea—a thin lemony butter wafer, dipped in or drizzled with semisweet chocolate.

Pictured on the cover.

Swedish Butter Cookies

½	**cup butter** *(not margarine)*
1	**cup all-purpose flour**
¼	**cup sugar**
1½	**teaspoons finely shredded lemon peel**
¼	**teaspoon vanilla**
4	**squares (4 ounces) semisweet chocolate**
2	**tablespoons shortening**

🍂 In a medium mixing bowl beat butter with an electric mixer on medium to high speed about 30 seconds or till softened.

🍂 Add about *half* of the flour to the butter. Then add the sugar, lemon peel, and vanilla. Beat on medium to high speed about 2 minutes or till thoroughly combined, scraping sides of bowl occasionally. Beat or stir in the remaining flour. Divide dough in half. Cover and chill about 1 hour or till dough is easy to handle.

🍂 On a lightly floured surface, roll *each* half of dough to ⅛-inch thickness.* Using 2-inch cutters, cut dough into desired shapes. Place 1-inch apart onto ungreased cookie sheets.

🍂 Bake in a 375° oven for 5 to 7 minutes or till bottoms are very lightly browned. Cool on cookie sheet for 1 minute. Remove cookies and cool on wire racks.

🍂 In a small heavy saucepan melt semisweet chocolate and shortening over low heat, stirring occasionally. Dip half of *each* cookie in the chocolate mixture. *Or,* drizzle chocolate mixture over cookies. Place on waxed paper and let stand about 30 minutes or till the chocolate is set. (If necessary, chill the cookies till the chocolate is set.) Makes about 80.

*Note: For thicker cookies, roll *each* half of dough to ¼-inch thickness and bake the cookies in the 375° oven for 7 to 9 minutes. Use 3 *squares* (3 ounces) semisweet chocolate and 4 *teaspoons* shortening for the chocolate mixture. Makes about 36.

Nutrition information per cookie: 27 calories, 0 g protein, 3 g carbohydrate, 2 g fat (1 g saturated), 3 mg cholesterol, 12 mg sodium, 8 mg potassium.

Luscious coffee-flavored buttercream sandwiched between two crisp and lacy wafers.

Swedish Lace Sandwich Cookies

½ **cup margarine *or* butter**
⅔ **cup sugar**
¼ **cup light corn syrup**
 2 **tablespoons water**
¾ **cup oat bran *(not cereal)***
½ **cup all-purpose flour**
½ **teaspoon ground cardamom**
¼ **teaspoon ground ginger**
¼ **teaspoon baking powder**
¼ **teaspoon baking soda**
 1 **teaspon vanilla**
    Coffee-Buttercream Frosting

🐢 Line cookie sheets with foil. Lightly spray with *nonstick spray coating*. Set aside.

🐢 In a saucepan melt margarine or butter over medium heat. Stir in sugar, syrup, and water till sugar is dissolved. Remove from heat.

🐢 In a bowl stir together the oat bran, flour, cardamom, ginger, baking powder, and baking soda. Add to syrup mixture with vanilla. Stir till thoroughly combined. Let stand 10 minutes.

🐢 Drop dough by level teaspoons about 2½ inches apart on the prepared cookie sheets. Bake in 375° oven for 5 to 7 minutes or till lightly browned. Cool on cookie sheets for 1 to 2 minutes. Remove and cool on wire racks.

🐢 To assemble, frost bottoms of *half* of the cookies with Coffee-Buttercream Frosting. Then top *each* with the remaining unfrosted cookies bottom sides down. Makes about 40.

Coffee-Buttercream Frosting: In a mixing bowl beat ¼ cup *margarine or butter* with an electric mixer on medium to high speed about 30 seconds or till softened. Gradually beat in 2 cups sifted *powdered sugar*. Beat in 2 tablespoons *milk* and 2 tablespoons *coffee-flavored liqueur* till smooth. Gradually beat in enough additional *powdered sugar* (about 1¼ cups) to make frosting of spreading consistency.

Nutrition information per cookie: 92 calories, 1 g protein, 15 g carbohydrate, 4 g fat (1 g saturated), 0 mg cholesterol, 49 mg sodium, 16 mg potassium.

71

Better Homes and Gardens®
COOKIES COOKIES COOKIES
Christmastime Treats

BETTER HOMES AND GARDENS® BOOKS
Des Moines, Iowa

Christmastime Treats

*W*hen cookies line the tables at bazaars and
well-wishers stop by your house with
holiday goodies, Christmastime is near. Bring
the spirit of Christmas into your home with an
assortment of festive, fresh-baked cookies
straight from your oven.

Cookie Recipes in this Book

Pictured on the cover: Almond Twists, Cranberry-Nut Pinwheels, Gumdrop Cookies, Gingerbread Cutouts, Layered Chocolate-Peanut Diamonds, Maple-Nut Bars, Roly-Poly Santas, Santa's Whiskers, Simple Snowflakes, Whole Wheat Spice Cookies (see recipe listing above for page numbers).

Merry Christmas Cookies

The perfect time to extend warm greetings to folks you've treasured throughout the year is during the Christmas season, when every day is laced with the spirit of giving. Share with them a selection of holiday-special cookies that you've baked and decorated with love.

Gumdrop Cookies
(see recipe, page 7)

Gingerbread Cutouts
(see recipe, page 56)

Savor the flavor of a cookie that's bursting with the goodness of fruit and nuts.

Cranberry-Oatmeal Drops

1 cup all-purpose flour
1 teaspoon baking powder
½ teaspoon ground cinnamon
¼ teaspoon ground nutmeg
½ cup margarine *or* butter
¾ cup packed brown sugar
1 egg
¼ cup milk
1 teaspoon finely shredded orange peel
1½ cups quick-cooking rolled oats
¾ cup chopped cranberries
¼ cup chopped walnuts *or* pecans
Orange Icing

In a medium mixing bowl stir together the flour, baking powder, cinnamon, and nutmeg. Set aside.

In a large mixing bowl beat the margarine or butter with an electric mixer on medium to high speed about 30 seconds or till softened.

Add the brown sugar and beat till fluffy. Then add the egg, milk, and orange peel. Beat till thoroughly combined, scraping the sides of the bowl occasionally. Add the flour mixture and beat till well mixed. Stir in the oats, cranberries, and walnuts or pecans.

Drop dough by tablespoons 2 inches apart onto greased cookie sheets. Bake in a 375° oven for 10 to 12 minutes or till lightly browned. Remove cookies and cool on wire racks. Drizzle with Orange Icing. Makes 28.

Orange Icing: In a small mixing bowl stir together 1 cup sifted *powdered sugar*, ½ teaspoon finely shredded *orange peel*, ¼ teaspoon *vanilla*, and enough *orange juice* (1 to 2 tablespoons) to make icing of drizzling consistency.

Nutrition information per cookie: 109 calories, 2 g protein, 16 g carbohydrate, 4 g fat (1 g saturated), 8 mg cholesterol, 54 mg sodium, 56 mg potassium.

Oh, what a treat! This cookie is brimming with holiday fancies like candied pineapple, dates, and nuts.

Fruit 'n' Almond Cookies

¾ cup margarine *or* butter
1¾ cups all-purpose flour
1 cup packed brown sugar
1 egg
½ teaspoon vanilla
½ teaspoon baking soda
⅛ teaspoon salt
¾ cup pitted whole dates, snipped
¾ cup candied pineapple, chopped
½ cup chopped almonds
⅓ cup whole almonds (optional)

🎁 In a large mixing bowl beat the magarine or butter with an electric mixer on medium to high speed about 30 seconds or till softened. Add about *half* of the flour to the margarine. Then add the brown sugar, egg, vanilla, baking soda, and salt. Beat till thoroughly combined, scraping the sides of the bowl occasionally. Beat in the remaining flour. Stir in the dates, candied pineapple, and chopped almonds.
🎁 Drop dough by rounded teaspoons 2 inches apart onto greased cookie sheets. If desired, place a whole almond in center of each cookie.
🎁 Bake in a 375° oven for 8 to 10 minutes or till lightly browned. Remove cookies and cool on wire racks. Makes 48.

Nutrition information per cookie: 83 calories, 1 g protein, 12 g carbohydrate, 4 g fat (1 g saturated), 4 mg cholesterol, 51 mg sodium, 51 mg potassium.

Purchased Shortbread Fix-Ups

🎁 As the hustle and bustle of the holiday season draws near and the days of cookie baking turn to a few, give these quick shortbread fix-ups a try.

Chocolate-Dipped Shortbread: Heat and stir ⅔ cup *semisweet chocolate pieces* and 1 tablespoon *shortening* over low heat till melted. Dip one corner of 40 square *shortbread cookies* into mixture. Sprinkle with ¼ cup finely chopped *pistachio nuts.* Place on waxed paper till set. Makes 40.

Peppermint Dips: Heat and stir 4 ounces *vanilla-flavored candy coating* and 1 tablespoon *shortening* over low heat till melted. Dip one corner of 40 square *shortbread cookies* into mixture. Sprinkle with ¼ cup crushed *peppermint candy.* Place on waxed paper till set. Makes 40.

If you really want these cookies to look Christmassy, only use red and green gumdrops.

Pictured on the cover and on page 4.

Gumdrop Cookies

¼ **cup shortening**
¼ **cup margarine** *or* **butter**
1 **cup all-purpose flour**
½ **cup sugar**
¼ **cup packed brown sugar**
1 **egg**
1 **teaspoon vanilla**
⅛ **teaspoon baking soda**
1 **cup gumdrops, snipped**

🎁 In a large mixing bowl beat the shortening and margarine or butter with an electric mixer on medium to high speed about 30 seconds or till softened. Add about *half* of the flour to the shortening mixture. Then add the sugar, brown sugar, egg, vanilla, and baking soda. Beat till thoroughly combined, scraping the sides of the bowl occasionally. Beat in the remaining flour. Stir in the gumdrops.
🎁 Drop by rounded teaspoons 2 inches apart onto ungreased cookie sheets. Bake in a 375° oven for 8 to 10 minutes or till edges are lightly browned. Cool on cookie sheets for 1 minute. Remove cookies and cool on wire racks. Makes about 36.

Nutrition information per cookie: 72 calories, 1 g protein, 11 g carbohydrate, 3 g fat (1 g saturated), 6 mg cholesterol, 22 mg sodium, 11 mg potassium.

Chocolate Confetti Cookies: Prepare Gumdrop Cookies as directed at left, *except* substitute 1 cup coarsely chopped *candy-coated milk chocolate pieces* for the snipped gumdrops.

Nutrition information per cookie: 81 calories, 1 g protein, 10 g carbohydrate, 4 g fat (1 g saturated), 6 mg cholesterol, 20 mg sodium, 11 mg potassium.

Discover all the flavors of fruitcake packed into these small pumpkin cookies.

Pumpkin-Fruit Drops

½ **cup margarine** *or* **butter**
1 **cup all-purpose flour**
1 **cup packed brown sugar**
1 **cup canned pumpkin**
1 **egg**
1 **teaspoon ground cinnamon**
1 **teaspoon vanilla**
½ **teaspoon baking powder**
½ **teaspoon baking soda**
¼ **teaspoon ground nutmeg**
¾ **cup toasted wheat germ**
¾ **cup chopped pecans**
¾ **cup raisins**
½ **cup chopped candied cherries**
Rum Glaze

In a large mixing bowl beat the margarine or butter with an electric mixer on medium to high speed about 30 seconds or till softened.

Add the flour, brown sugar, pumpkin, egg, cinnamon, vanilla, baking powder, baking soda, and nutmeg. Beat till thoroughly combined, scraping sides of bowl occasionally. Then beat or stir in the wheat germ. Stir in the pecans, raisins, and candied cherries.

Drop dough by rounded teaspoons 2 inches apart onto greased cookie sheets. Bake in a 375° oven for 10 to 12 minutes or till edges are firm. Remove cookies and cool on wire racks. Drizzle with Rum Glaze. Makes about 48.

Rum Glaze: In a small mixing bowl stir together 1 cup sifted *powdered sugar*, 1 teaspoon *rum*, and enough *milk* (about 3 teaspoons) to make glaze of drizzling consistency.

Nutrition information per cookie: 86 calories, 1 g protein, 13 g carbohydrate, 3 g fat (1 g saturated), 4 mg cholesterol, 38 mg sodium, 72 mg potassium.

In a large mixing bowl beat the margarine or butter with an electric mixer on medium to high speed about 30 seconds or till softened. Add *half* of the flour to the margarine. Then add the sugar, egg, milk, and vanilla. Beat till thoroughly combined, scraping the sides of bowl occasionally. Then beat or stir in the remaining flour. Stir in the 1 cup coconut.

Drop dough by rounded teaspoons 2 inches apart onto ungreased cookie sheets.
Bake in a 375° oven for 8 to 10 minutes or till edges are firm and bottoms are lightly browned. Remove cookies and cool on wire racks. Spread Pink Frosting on top of cookies. Sprinkle with toasted coconut. Makes 24.

Extend a holiday greeting to neighbors with a plate of these delicious coconut-capped cookies.

Coconut Jumbles

½ **cup margarine *or* butter**
1½ **cups all-purpose flour**
¾ **cup sugar**
1 **egg**
3 **tablespoons milk**
1 **teaspoon vanilla**
1 **cup coconut**
   Pink Frosting
   Toasted coconut

Pink Frosting: Combine 2 cups sifted *powdered sugar*, a few drops *red food coloring*, and enough *milk* (1 to 2 tablespoons) to make frosting of spreading consistency.

Nutrition information per cookie: 143 calories, 1 g protein, 22 g carbohydrate, 6 g fat (2 g saturated), 9 mg cholesterol, 53 mg sodium, 32 mg potassium.

9

Chocolate kisses—an unbeatable sweetness to complement the tangy cranberries in these cookies.

Chocolate-Cranberry Cookies

½ **cup margarine** *or* **butter**
1 **cup all-purpose flour**
¾ **cup sugar**
1 **egg**
1 **teaspoon vanilla**
½ **teaspoon baking powder**
1 **cup quick-cooking rolled oats**
1 **cup coarsely chopped cranberries**
½ **cup finely chopped walnuts** *or* **pecans**
42 **milk-chocolate kisses**

 In a large mixing bowl beat the margarine or butter with an electric mixer on medium to high speed about 30 seconds or till softened.

Add the flour, sugar, egg, vanilla, and baking powder. Beat till thoroughly combined, scraping the sides of the bowl occasionally. Stir in the rolled oats, cranberries, and walnuts or pecans.
 Drop by rounded teaspoons 1 inch apart onto greased cookie sheets. Place a chocolate kiss in center of each cookie.
 Bake in a 375° oven for 10 to 12 minutes or till edges are lightly browned. Remove cookies and cool on wire racks. Makes 42.

Nutrition information per cookie: 87 calories, 1 g protein, 10 g carbohydrate, 5 g fat (1 g saturated), 6 mg cholesterol, 35 mg sodium, 37 mg potassium.

Each irresistible cookie has a crisp, candylike texture and a thin layer of chocolate.

Apricot Florentines

6 tablespoons margarine *or* butter
⅓ cup evaporated milk
¼ cup sugar
2 tablespoons honey
1 cup sliced almonds
½ cup snipped dried apricots
¼ cup light raisins
¼ cup all-purpose flour
¾ cup semisweet chocolate pieces
2 tablespoons shortening

🎁 In a medium saucepan combine the margarine or butter, evaporated milk, sugar, and honey. Bring to a full rolling boil, stirring occasionally. Remove from heat. Stir in the almonds, apricots, and raisins. Stir in the flour.

🎁 Drop by level tablespoons at least 3 inches apart onto *greased and floured* cookie sheets. (Grease and flour cookie sheets for each batch.) Using the back of a spoon, spread the batter into 3-inch circles.

🎁 Bake in a 350° oven about 8 minutes or till edges are lightly browned. Cool on cookie sheets for 1 minute, then carefully transfer cookies to waxed paper. Cool thoroughly.

🎁 In a small heavy saucepan melt the chocolate pieces and shortening over low heat, stirring occasionally. Spread about *1 teaspoon* of the chocolate mixture evenly over the *bottom* of each cookie. When chocolate is almost set, draw crisscross lines through it with the tines of a fork. Store, covered, in the refrigerator with a sheet of waxed paper between layers. Makes about 24.

Nutrition information per cookie: 126 calories, 2 g protein, 12 g carbohydrate, 9 g fat (1 g saturated), 1 mg cholesterol, 38 mg sodium, 119 mg potassium.

Sprinkle on the ground mace just as soon as you're done brushing on the glaze. That way, the mace is sure to stay.

Lemon-Mace Cookies

½ **cup margarine** *or* **butter**
2 **cups all-purpose flour**
1 **cup sugar**
½ **cup dairy sour cream** *or* **buttermilk**
1 **egg**
2 **teaspoons finely shredded lemon peel**
1 **teaspoon baking powder**
¼ **teaspoon baking soda**
½ **teaspoon ground mace**
  Lemon Glaze
  Ground mace

In a large mixing bowl beat the margarine or butter with an electric mixer on medium to high speed about 30 seconds or till softened. Add about *half* of the flour to the margarine.

Then add the sugar, sour cream or buttermilk, egg, lemon peel, baking powder, baking soda, and mace. Beat on low speed till thoroughly combined, scraping the sides of the bowl occasionally. Then beat on medium speed for 1 minute. Beat in the remaining flour.

Drop by rounded teaspoons 2 inches apart onto ungreased cookie sheets. Bake in a 375° oven for 8 to 10 minutes or till edges are lightly browned. Remove cookies and cool on wire racks. While still warm, brush with Lemon Glaze. Sprinkle with mace. Makes about 36.

Lemon Glaze: In a small bowl stir together ¼ cup *sugar* and 2 tablespoons *lemon juice*.

Nutrition information per cookie: 80 calories, 1 g protein, 12 g carbohydrate, 3 g fat (1 g saturated), 7 mg cholesterol, 48 mg sodium, 16 mg potassium.

All-Fruit Mincemeat

4 cups chopped unpeeled apples
2 cups raisins, chopped
1 cup snipped dried apricots
1 6-ounce can (¾ cup) frozen apple juice
    concentrate, thawed
¾ cup water
¼ cup honey
1 teaspoon ground allspice
½ teaspoon salt
2 tablespoons brandy

In a 4½-quart Dutch oven stir together the apples, raisins, apricots, apple juice concentrate, water, honey, allspice, and salt. Bring to boiling, reduce heat. Cover and simmer for 50 minutes, stirring occasionally. Uncover and simmer for 10 to 15 minutes more or till liquid has nearly evaporated, stirring occasionally. Stir in the brandy. Cool. Store, covered, in the refrigerator. Makes about 8 cups.

Nutrition information per cup: 265 calories, 2 g protein, 67 g carbohydrate, 1 g fat (0 g saturated), 0 mg cholesterol, 147 mg sodium, 686 mg potassium.

Mincemeat Drop Cookies

1 cup margarine *or* butter
3 cups all-purpose flour
1 cup sugar
2 eggs
1 teaspoon baking powder
¼ teaspoon baking soda
2 cups All-Fruit Mincemeat (see recipe,
    left) *or* prepared mincemeat
½ cup chopped walnuts *or* pecans
    Brandy Icing

In a large mixing bowl beat the margarine or butter with an electric mixer on medium to high speed about 30 seconds or till softened. Add *half* the flour to the margarine. Then add the sugar, eggs, baking powder, and baking soda. Beat till thoroughly combined, scraping the sides of the bowl occasionally. Beat in the remaining flour. Stir in the All-Fruit Mincemeat or prepared mincemeat and walnuts or pecans.
Drop dough by rounded teaspoons about 2 inches apart onto greased cookie sheets. Bake in a 350° oven for 11 to 13 minutes or till lightly browned. Cool on cookie sheets for 1 minute. Remove cookies; cool on wire racks. Drizzle with Brandy Icing. Makes about 72.

Brandy Icing: In a small mixing bowl stir together 2 cups sifted *powdered sugar*, 1 tablespoon *brandy*, and enough *milk* (2 to 3 tablespoons) to make of drizzling consistency.

Nutrition information per cookie: 75 calories, 1 g protein, 11 g carbohydrate, 3 g fat (1 g saturated), 0 mg cholesterol, 42 mg sodium, 30 mg potassium.

In a medium saucepan melt the margarine or butter and unsweetened chocolate over low heat, stirring frequently. Remove from heat. Add the sugar, eggs, and vanilla. Using a wooden spoon, *lightly* beat just till combined (*don't overbeat* or brownies will rise too high, then fall). Stir in the flour.

Spread the batter into a greased 9x9x2-inch baking pan. Sprinkle chopped mint candies over batter. Bake in a 350° oven for 27 minutes. Cool in pan on a wire rack.

Place Green Frosting in a decorating bag fitted with a a small plain tip. Spread Chocolate Glaze over brownies. Immediately pipe Green Frosting in lines about ¾ inch apart on top of glaze. Run a toothpick, skewer, or knife blade across green lines, cleaning tip frequently. Let frosting set 1 hour. Cut into bars. Makes 24.

Green Frosting: In a small bowl stir together ½ cup sifted *powdered sugar*, 1 teaspoon *milk*, and 1 small drop *green food coloring* till well combined.

Chocolate Glaze: In a small bowl stir together 1 cup sifted *powdered sugar*, 2 tablespoons *unsweetened cocoa powder*, ¼ teaspoon *vanilla*, and enough *milk* (1½ to 2 tablespoons) to make of glazing consistency.

Nutrition information per bar: 133 calories, 1 g protein, 20 g carbohydrate, 6 g fat (1 g saturated), 18 mg cholesterol, 51 mg sodium, 37 mg potassium.

If you don't have the time for fancy decorating, omit the Green Frosting. Instead, top each brownie with half of a layered chocolate-mint candy.

Mint Brownies

½   **cup margarine *or* butter**
2   **squares (2 ounces) unsweetened chocolate**
1   **cup sugar**
2   **eggs**
1   **teaspoon vanilla**
¾   **cup all-purpose flour**
18   **layered chocolate-mint candies, chopped**
    Green Frosting
    Chocolate Glaze

14

Making even diamonds is easy. Just measure bars with a ruler and mark with toothpicks before cutting.

Pictured on the cover.

Layered Chocolate-Peanut Diamonds

⅓ **cup margarine *or* butter**
¼ **cup peanut butter**
1¼ **cups all-purpose flour**
¾ **cup packed brown sugar**
1 **8-ounce package cream cheese, softened**
¼ **cup honey**
2 **tablespoons all-purpose flour**
2 **tablespoons brown sugar**
2 **eggs**
1½ **cups finely chopped peanuts**
1 **6-ounce package (1 cup) semisweet chocolate pieces**

For crust, in a small mixing bowl beat the margarine or butter and peanut butter with an electric mixer on medium to high speed for 30 seconds. Add about *half* of the 1¼ cups flour to the margarine mixture. Then add the ¾ cup brown sugar. Beat till thoroughly combined, scraping the sides of the bowl occasionally. Beat or stir in the remaining half of the 1¼ cups flour.

Press mixture into the bottom of an ungreased 13x9x2-inch baking dish. Bake in a 350° oven about 15 minutes or till lightly browned.

Meanwhile, in a small mixing bowl combine the cream cheese, honey, the 2 tablespoons flour, and 2 tablespoons brown sugar. Beat on medium speed till combined. Add the eggs and beat just till combined. Stir in *1 cup* of the peanuts. Pour over the partially baked crust. Bake in a 350° oven about 15 minutes more or till set.

Sprinkle chocolate pieces over top. Bake about 2 minutes more or till chocolate is softened. Place the dish on a wire rack. Spread melted chocolate pieces evenly over the top. Sprinkle with remaining peanuts. Cool thoroughly in pan on a wire rack. Cut into diamonds or squares. Store, covered, in the refrigerator. Makes 42.

Nutrition information per bar: 130 calories, 3 g protein, 13 g carbohydrate, 8 g fat (2 g saturated), 16 mg cholesterol, 45 mg sodium, 90 mg potassium.

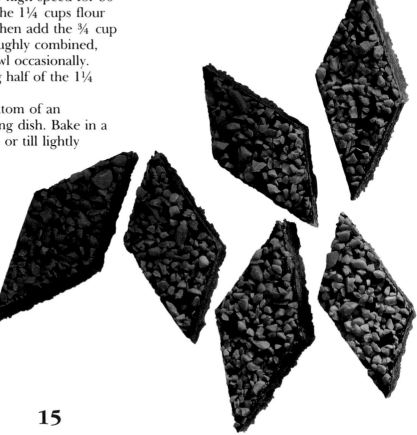

Shh... here's a secret. Mint-flavored chocolate pieces are nestled in the center of these chocolaty brownies.

Peppermint Stick Brownies

1½ cups all-purpose flour
½ teaspoon baking powder
½ teaspoon baking soda
1¼ cups sugar
¾ cup margarine *or* butter
½ cup unsweetened cocoa powder
2 eggs
1 teaspoon vanilla
1 cup milk
¾ cup mint-flavored chocolate pieces
1 cup chopped walnuts *or* pecans
Fudge Frosting
½ cup broken peppermint sticks *or* coarsely crushed striped round peppermint candies

In a medium bowl stir together the flour, baking powder, and baking soda. Set aside.

In a large saucepan combine the sugar, margarine or butter, and cocoa powder. Cook over medium heat till margarine melts, stirring constantly. Remove from heat. Add eggs and vanilla. Using a wooden spoon, *lightly* beat just till combined (*don't overbeat*).

Add the flour mixture and milk alternately to the chocolate mixture, beating after each addition. Stir in the chocolate pieces and walnuts or pecans. Spread batter into a greased 15x10x1-inch baking pan.

Bake in a 350° oven for 20 to 25 minutes or till a wooden toothpick inserted near center comes out clean. Cool in pan on a wire rack. Frost with Fudge Frosting. Sprinkle with crushed peppermint. Cut into bars. Makes 48.

Fudge Frosting: In a small heavy saucepan melt 2 squares (2 ounces) *unsweetened chocolate* and ¼ cup *margarine or butter* over low heat, stirring occasionally. Remove from heat. Stir in 3⅓ cups sifted *powdered sugar* and 1 teaspoon *vanilla*. Stir in enough *hot water* (2 to 4 tablespoons) to make a soft spreading consistency.

Nutrition information per bar: 147 calories, 2 g protein, 20 g carbohydrate, 7 g fat (1 g saturated), 9 mg cholesterol, 63 mg sodium, 48 mg potassium.

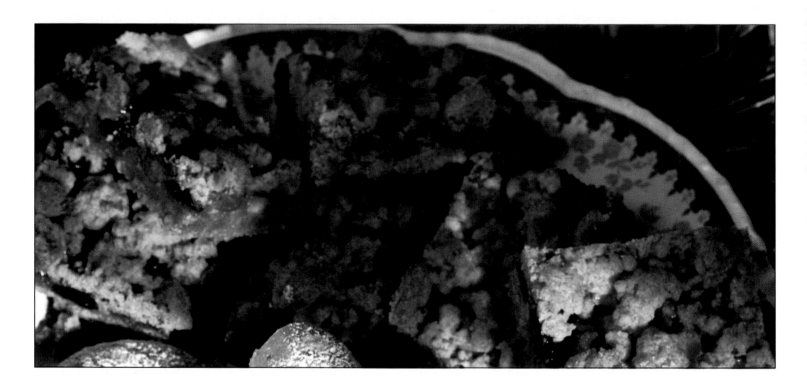

Two tips for easy cutting: One, line the pan with foil, extending the foil over the edges. After the bars cool, lift the foil out—bars and all. Peel off the foil and discard. Two, use a sharp knife to help avoid crumbling.

Brandied Fruit Bars

1 **cup mixed dried fruit bits**
¼ **cup brandy** *or* **apple juice**
1 **cup whole wheat flour**
¾ **cup all-purpose flour**
½ **cup finely chopped pecans**
¾ **cup margarine** *or* **butter**
½ **cup packed brown sugar**
⅓ **cup apricot preserves** *or* **orange marmalade**

In a small saucepan combine the fruit bits and brandy or apple juice. Carefully bring to boiling; reduce heat. Simmer, covered, for 3 to 5 minutes or till liquid is absorbed.

Meanwhile, in a medium bowl stir together whole wheat flour, all-purpose flour, and pecans. Set aside.

In a large mixing bowl beat the margarine or butter with an electric mixer on medium to high speed about 30 seconds or till softened. Add the brown sugar and beat till fluffy, scraping the sides of the bowl occasionally. Add flour mixture and continue to beat till crumbly. Reserve *1 cup* of the crumb mixture. Press remaining crumb mixture into the bottom of an ungreased 9x9x2-inch baking pan.

Stir preserves or marmalade into fruit bits. Spread mixture atop crumb mixture in pan. Sprinkle with reserved crumbs. Lightly press the crumbs into fruit layer.

Bake in a 375° oven for 20 to 25 minutes or till crumbs are lightly browned. Cool in pan on a wire rack. Cut into bars. Makes 24.

Nutrition information per bar: 146 calories, 1 g protein, 18 g carbohydrate, 7 g fat (1 g saturated), 0 mg cholesterol, 73 mg sodium, 97 mg potassium.

Cranberry-Pecan Bars

Make several batches of these bars during cranberry season, freeze them, and keep them on hand for holiday company and gift giving.

1 cup all-purpose flour
2 tablespoons sugar
⅓ cup margarine *or* butter
½ cup finely chopped pecans
1¼ cups sugar
2 tablespoons all-purpose flour
2 beaten eggs
2 tablespoons milk
1 tablespoon finely shredded orange peel
1 teaspoon vanilla
1 cup chopped cranberries
½ cup coconut
½ cup finely chopped pecans

For crust, in a medium mixing bowl combine the 1 cup flour and the 2 tablespoons sugar. Using a pastry blender, cut in the margarine or butter till mixture resembles coarse crumbs.

Stir in ½ cup pecans. Press flour mixture into the bottom of an ungreased 13x9x2-inch baking pan. Bake in a 350° oven for 15 minutes.

Meanwhile, in a large mixing bowl combine the 1¼ cups sugar and the 2 tablespoons flour. Stir in the eggs, milk, orange peel, and vanilla. Fold in the cranberries, coconut, and ½ cup pecans. Spread over partially baked crust. Bake in a 350° oven for 25 to 30 minutes more or till top is lightly browned. Cool in pan on a wire rack. While still warm, cut into bars. Cool completely. Makes 36.

Nutrition information per bar: 87 calories, 1 g protein, 12 g carbohydrate, 4 g fat (1 g saturated), 12 mg cholesterol, 24 mg sodium, 27 mg potassium.

Relish the goodness of the wonderful blend of spices in these cakey iced bars.

Spicy Holiday Fruit Bars

2 cups all-purpose flour
1 teaspoon ground cinnamon
½ teaspoon ground ginger
½ teaspoon baking soda
½ teaspoon ground nutmeg
¼ teaspoon ground cloves
¼ teaspoon ground allspice
½ cup shortening
½ cup packed brown sugar
¾ cup buttermilk
⅓ cup molasses
1 egg
½ cup chopped nuts
⅓ cup raisins, chopped dates, dried cherries, *or* dried cranberries
⅓ cup chopped mixed candied fruit and peels
Orange Icing
Additional mixed candied fruit and peels (optional)

In a large mixing bowl stir together the flour, cinnamon, ginger, baking soda, nutmeg, cloves, and allspice. Set aside.

In a large mixing bowl beat the shortening with an electric mixer on medium to high speed for 30 seconds. Add the brown sugar and beat till fluffy. Add the buttermilk, molasses, and egg. Gradually add flour mixture, beating till thoroughly combined. Stir in the nuts, raisins, and ⅓ cup candied fruit.

Spread into a greased 15x10x1-inch baking pan. Bake in a 350° oven for 15 to 20 minutes or till lightly browned. Cool thoroughly in pan on a wire rack. Frost with Orange Icing. If desired, decorate with additional candied fruit and peels. Cut into bars. Makes 48.

Orange Icing: In a small mixing bowl stir together 2 cups sifted *powdered sugar*, 1 teaspoon finely shredded *orange peel*, ½ teaspoon *vanilla*, and enough *orange juice* (about 2 tablespoons) to make icing of spreading consistency.

Nutrition information per bar: 85 calories, 1 g protein, 13 g carbohydrate, 3 g fat (1 g saturated), 5 mg cholesterol, 15 mg sodium, 56 mg potassium.

If you didn't know better, you'd think you were eating a rich and delicious pumpkin bar.

Sweet Potato-Cheesecake Bars

⅔ **cup finely crushed graham crackers**
½ **cup all-purpose flour**
½ **cup finely chopped peanuts**
¼ **cup sugar**
½ **cup margarine *or* butter, melted**
1 **8-ounce can sweet potatoes, drained**
½ **of an 8-ounce package cream cheese, softened**
⅓ **cup sugar**
¾ **teaspoon pumpkin pie spice**
1 **egg**
½ **cup dairy sour cream**
1 **tablespoon milk**
2 **tablespoons finely chopped peanuts**

❖ For crust, in a medium mixing bowl stir together the finely crushed graham crackers, flour, ½ cup peanuts, and ¼ cup sugar. Add the melted margarine or butter and mix well.
❖ Press mixture into the bottom of an ungreased 9x9x2-inch baking pan. Bake in a 350° oven for 12 minutes.

❖ Meanwhile, in small mixing bowl combine the sweet potatoes, cream cheese, ⅓ cup sugar, and pumpkin pie spice. Beat with an electric mixer on medium speed till thoroughly combined, scraping the sides of the bowl occasionally. Add egg. Beat just till combined. Stir in the sour cream and milk just till combined. Pour over partially baked crust. Sprinkle with 2 tablespoons peanuts.
❖ Bake in 350° oven about 20 minutes or till a knife inserted off-center comes out clean. Cool in pan on a wire rack. Cut into bars. Store, covered, in the refrigerator. Makes 36.

Nutrition information per bar: 88 calories, 2 g protein, 8 g carbohydrate, 6 g fat (2 g saturated), 11 mg cholesterol, 55 mg sodium, 58 mg potassium.

It's magic! Substitute light corn syrup for the maple-flavored syrup and pecans for the walnuts, and presto! You have pecan pie bars.

Pictured on the cover.

Maple-Nut Bars

1½ **cups all-purpose flour**
 2 **tablespoons brown sugar**
 ½ **cup margarine** *or* **butter**
 2 **eggs**
 ½ **cup packed brown sugar**
 ½ **cup chopped walnuts**
 ½ **cup maple-flavored syrup**
 2 **tablespoons margarine** *or* **butter, melted**
 1 **teaspoon vanilla**

🎁 For crust, in a large mixing bowl stir together the flour and 2 tablespoons brown sugar. Using a pastry blender, cut in ½ cup magarine or butter till crumbly. Press mixture into the bottom of an ungreased 11x7½x2-inch baking pan. Bake in 350° oven for 15 minutes.
🎁 Meanwhile, for nut layer, in another mixing bowl use a fork to beat eggs slightly. Stir in ½ cup brown sugar, walnuts, maple-flavored syrup, 2 tablespoons melted margarine or butter, and vanilla.
🎁 Pour the nut mixture over the partially baked layer. Bake in a 350° oven for 25 minutes more or till set. Slightly cool in pan on a wire rack. Cut into bars. Store, covered, in the refrigerator. Makes 32.

Nutrition information per bar: 98 calories, 1 g protein, 12 g carbohydrate, 5 g fat (1 g saturated), 13 mg cholesterol, 50 mg sodium, 36 mg potassium.

Festive Bar Shapes

🎁 Looking for some new ways to vary the shape of your bar cookies? Here are some easy ideas to try.

For triangles, cut cookie bars into 2- to 2½-inch squares. Then, diagonally cut each of the squares in half.

For diamonds, first make straight parallel cuts 1 to 1½ inches apart down the length of the pan. Then, make diagonal cuts across the straight cuts 1 to 1½ inches apart, forming a diamond pattern.

Baklava

4 **cups (1 pound) walnuts, finely chopped**
½ **cup sugar**
1 **teaspoon ground cinnamon**
1¼ **cups margarine *or* butter, melted**
1 **16-ounce package frozen phyllo dough, thawed**
1½ **cups sugar**
1 **cup water**
¼ **cup honey**
½ **teaspoon finely shredded lemon peel**
2 **tablespoons lemon juice**
2 **inches stick cinnamon**

ⵌ For filling, stir together chopped walnuts, ½ cup sugar, and ground cinnamon. Set aside.
ⵌ Brush the bottom of a 15x10x1-inch baking pan with some of the melted margarine or butter. Unfold phyllo. Layer about *one-fourth* of the phyllo sheets in the pan, brushing each sheet generously with melted margarine and allowing phyllo to extend up the sides of the pan. Sprinkle about *1½ cups* of the filling over the phyllo in the pan. Repeat layering phyllo and filling 2 more times.

ⵌ Layer remaining phyllo sheets in the pan, brushing each sheet with margarine. Drizzle any remaining margarine over top layer. Trim edges of phyllo to fit pan. Using a sharp knife, cut through all layers to make triangle- or diamond-shaped pieces or squares. Bake in a 325° oven for 45 to 50 minutes or till lightly browned. Slightly cool in pan on a wire rack.
ⵌ Meanwhile, in a medium saucepan stir together 1½ cups sugar, water, honey, lemon peel, lemon juice, and stick cinnamon. Bring to boiling; reduce heat. Simmer, uncovered, for 20 minutes. Remove cinnamon. Pour honey mixture over warm baklava in the pan. Cool completely. Makes about 60.

Nutrition information per bar: 132 calories, 2 g protein, 14 g carbohydrate, 8 g fat (1 g saturated), 0 mg cholesterol, 72 mg sodium, 48 mg potassium.

Whole Wheat Spice Cookies

You can make one cookie recipe look like several batches. Dip some cookies in Sugar Glaze, drizzle some with Chocolate Glaze, and sprinkle others with nuts or chocolate-flavored sprinkles.

Pictured on the cover.

1	**cup margarine** *or* **butter**
1½	**cups all-purpose flour**
½	**cup sugar**
½	**cup packed brown sugar**
1	**egg white**
1	**teaspoon ground cinnamon**
¼	**teaspoon ground cloves**
¼	**teaspoon ground allspice** *or* **ground nutmeg**
¾	**cup whole wheat flour**
	Sugar Glaze *and/or* **Chocolate Glaze**

♟ In a large mixing bowl beat the margarine or butter with an electric mixer on medium to high speed about 30 seconds or till softened. Add the all-purpose flour to the margarine. Then add the sugar, brown sugar, egg white, cinnamon, cloves, and allspice or nutmeg. Beat till thoroughly combined, scraping the sides of the bowl occasionally. Then beat or stir in the whole wheat flour.

♟ Shape the dough into two 7-inch rolls. Wrap each in waxed paper or plastic wrap. Chill for 4 to 48 hours.

♟ Cut the chilled dough into ¼-inch-thick slices. Place slices 1 inch apart onto ungreased cookie sheets. Bake in a 375° oven about 8 minutes or till lightly browned. Remove cookies and cool on wire racks.

♟ To decorate, dip or drizzle cookies with Sugar Glaze and/or Chocolate Glaze. Place on waxed paper. If desired, immediately top with walnuts or chocolate-flavored sprinkles. Let stand till glaze is set. Makes about 54.

Sugar Glaze: In a small mixing bowl stir together 2 cups sifted *powdered sugar,* 1 tablespoon light *corn syrup,* and enough *milk* (2 to 3 tablespoons) to make glaze of drizzling consistency.

Chocolate Glaze: In a small heavy saucepan melt one 6-ounce package (1 cup) *semisweet chocolate pieces* and 2 tablespoons *shortening* over low heat, stirring occasionally.

Nutrition information per cookie: 78 calories, 1 g protein, 11 g carbohydrate, 3 g fat (1 g saturated), 0 mg cholesterol, 42 mg sodium, 21 mg potassium.

Here are pinwheel cookies that are just as pretty as can be. Their deep red cranberry swirls sparkle on a tray like jewels in a treasure chest.

Pictured on the cover.

Cranberry-Nut Pinwheels

1 cup cranberries
½ cup sugar
1 teaspoon cornstarch
¼ cup water
⅔ cup cashews
2 tablespoons margarine *or* butter, softened
¾ cup margarine *or* butter
3 cups all-purpose flour
1 cup sugar
1 egg
3 tablespoons milk
½ teaspoon baking soda
½ teaspoon vanilla

For filling, in a small saucepan combine the cranberries, ½ cup sugar, and cornstarch. Add water. Bring to boiling, stirring to dissolve the sugar. Boil gently over medium heat for 5 minutes, stirring frequently. Remove from heat. Press the hot mixture through a sieve. Discard the solids. Cover the surface of the hot mixture and cool without stirring.

Place the cashews in a blender container or food processer bowl. Cover and blend or process till finely ground. Add the 2 tablespoons margarine or butter. Cover and blend or process about 3 minutes more or till mixture is smooth and spreadable. Stop and scrape down sides as necessary.

In a large mixing bowl beat the ¾ cup margarine or butter and cashew mixture with an electric mixer on medium to high speed about 30 seconds or till softened. Add about *half* of the flour to the margarine mixture. Then add the 1 cup sugar, egg, milk, baking soda, and vanilla. Beat till thoroughly combined, scraping the sides of the bowl occasionally. Then beat or stir in the remaining flour. Cover and chill about 1 hour or till easy to handle.

Divide dough in half. Place *each* half of the dough between 2 sheets of waxed paper. Using a rolling pin, roll *each* half into a 16x12-inch rectangle.

Spread filling over *each* half of dough. From a short side, roll up each half jelly-roll style, removing waxed paper as you roll. Moisten and pinch edges to seal. Wrap each in waxed paper or plastic wrap. Chill for 4 to 48 hours.

Cut dough into ¼-inch-thick slices. Place about 2 inches apart onto greased cookie sheets. (If you wish, place some cookies in pairs, with edges touching.)

Bake in a 375° oven for 10 to 12 minutes or till edges are firm and bottoms are lightly browned. Remove cookies and cool on wire racks. Makes about 96 single pinwheels or about 48 double pinwheels.

Nutrition information per cookie: 46 calories, 1 g protein, 6 g carbohydrate, 2 g fat (0 g saturated), 2 mg cholesterol, 25 mg sodium, 12 mg potassium.

Gently roll the cookie-dough rolls on a flat surface several times during chilling to ensure their perfect pinwheel shape.

Chocolate-Mint Pinwheels

½ **cup shortening**
½ **cup margarine *or* butter**
1 **cup sugar**
1 **egg**
2 **tablespoons milk**
1 **teaspoon vanilla**
2¾ **cups all-purpose flour**
½ **teaspoon baking powder**
¼ **teaspoon salt**
½ **teaspoon mint extract**
¼ **teaspoon green food coloring**
¼ **cup unsweetened cocoa powder**

In a large mixing bowl beat shortening and margarine or butter with an electric mixer on medium to high speed about 30 seconds or till softened. Add the sugar and beat till fluffy. Add the egg, milk, and vanilla. Beat till thoroughly combined, scraping the sides of the bowl occasionally. Divide mixture in half.

In a medium bowl stir together the flour, baking powder, and salt. Into one portion of the shortening mixture stir *1½ cups* of the flour mixture, mint extract, and food coloring. Stir the cocoa powder into remaining flour mixture.

Add cocoa mixture to the remaining shortening mixture and mix well.

Place *each* portion between 2 sheets of waxed paper. Using a rolling pin, roll *each* portion into a 12x11-inch rectangle. Invert the green dough on top of the chocolate dough. Peel off top sheet of paper. From a long side, roll up jelly-roll style, removing waxed paper as you roll. Cut roll crosswise in half. Wrap each half in waxed paper or plastic wrap. Chill for 4 to 48 hours.

Cut chilled dough into ¼-inch-thick slices. Place 2 inches apart onto ungreased cookie sheets.

Bake in a 375° oven for 8 to 10 minutes or till edges are firm and bottoms are lightly browned. Remove cookies and cool on wire racks. Makes about 48.

Nutrition information per cookie: 78 calories, 1 g protein, 9 g carbohydrate, 4 g fat (1 g saturated), 4 mg cholesterol, 39 mg sodium, 33 mg potassium.

Share these mincemeat treasures with your guests anytime between Thanksgiving and Christmas.

Mincemeat Swirls

 2 **cups all-purpose flour**
 ½ **teaspoon baking powder**
 ¼ **teaspoon baking soda**
 ½ **cup shortening**
 1 **cup packed brown sugar**
 1 **egg**
 ½ **teaspoon vanilla**
 1½ **cups All-Fruit Mincemeat, drained (see recipe, page 13),** *or* **1½ cups prepared mincemeat plus 1 teaspoon finely shredded lemon peel** *or* **orange peel**
 ½ **cup finely chopped nuts**

🎁 In a medium bowl stir together the flour, baking powder, and baking soda. Set aside.
🎁 In a large mixing bowl beat the shortening with an electric mixer on medium to high speed for 30 seconds. Add the brown sugar and beat till fluffy. Add the egg and vanilla. Beat till thoroughly combined, scraping the sides of bowl occasionally. Add dry ingredients and beat well. Cover and chill for 30 minutes.

🎁 For filling, stir together the All-Fruit Mincemeat and nuts or the prepared mincemeat, lemon or orange peel, and nuts.
🎁 Divide dough in half. Place *each* half of the dough between 2 sheets of waxed paper. Using a rolling pin, roll *each* half into a 12x8-inch rectangle.
🎁 Spread filling over *each* half of the dough. From a short side, roll each half up jelly-roll style, removing waxed paper as you roll. Moisten and pinch edges to seal. Wrap each in waxed paper or plastic wrap. Chill for 4 to 48 hours.
🎁 Cut the chilled dough into ¼-inch-thick slices. Place 2 inches apart onto greased cookie sheets. Bake in a 350° oven for 8 to 10 minutes or till edges are firm and bottoms are lightly browned. Remove cookies and cool on wire racks. Makes about 60.

Nutrition information per cookie: 57 calories,
1 g protein, 8 g carbohydrate, 2 g fat (1 g saturated),
4 mg cholesterol, 12 mg sodium, 40 mg potassium.

Coconut wrapped around each cherry-filled cookie is reminiscent of Santa's whiskers.

Pictured on the cover.

Santa's Whiskers

¾ **cup margarine *or* butter**
2 **cups all-purpose flour**
¾ **cup sugar**
1 **tablespoon milk**
1 **teaspoon vanilla**
¾ **cup finely chopped candied red *or* green cherries**
⅓ **cup finely chopped pecans**
¾ **cup coconut**

🎁 In a large mixing bowl beat the margarine or butter with an electric mixer on medium to high speed about 30 seconds or till softened. Add about *half* of the flour to the margarine. Then add the sugar, milk, and vanilla. Beat till thoroughly combined, scraping the sides of the bowl occasionally. Then beat or stir in the remaining flour. Stir in the candied cherries and pecans.
🎁 Shape the dough into two 8-inch rolls. Roll in coconut. Wrap each in waxed paper or plastic wrap. Chill for 4 to 48 hours.
🎁 Cut the chilled dough into ¼-inch-thick slices. Place 1 inch apart onto ungreased cookie sheets.
🎁 Bake in a 375° oven for 10 to 12 minutes or till edges are lightly browned. Remove cookies and cool on wire racks. Makes about 60.

Nutrition information per cookie: 58 calories, 1 g protein, 7 g carbohydrate, 3 g fat (1 g saturated), 0 mg cholesterol, 27 mg sodium, 11 mg potassium.

Crisp, sugar-edged cookies with colorful candy clappers.

Anise Bells

¾ **cup margarine** *or* **butter**
¼ **teaspoon salt**
⅔ **cup sugar**
1 **egg**
¼ **teaspoon anise extract** *or* **coconut flavoring**
1¾ **cups all-purpose flour**
Red *or* **green colored sugar**
Red and green candy-coated milk chocolate pieces

🎁 In a large mixing bowl beat the margarine or butter and salt with an electric mixer on medium to high speed about 30 seconds or till softened. Add the sugar and beat till fluffy. Add the egg and anise extract or coconut flavoring. Beat till thoroughly combined, scraping the sides of the bowl occasionally. Add the flour and beat till well mixed. Cover and chill about 30 minutes or till easy to handle.

🎁 Divide dough in half. Shape dough into two 6-inch rolls. Roll in colored sugar. Wrap each in waxed paper or plastic wrap. Chill for 4 to 48 hours.

🎁 Cut the chilled dough into ¼-inch-thick slices. Place slices about 2 inches apart onto ungreased cookie sheets. Place a milk chocolate piece on the bottom half of each slice for a bell clapper. Let slices stand for 1 to 2 minutes to soften for easier handling. Fold in sides of each slice, overlapping at top and slightly covering candy.

🎁 Bake in a 350° oven for 10 to 12 minutes or till edges and bottoms are very lightly browned. Remove cookies and cool on wire racks. Makes about 48.

Nutrition information per cookie: 62 calories, 1 g protein, 8 g carbohydrate, 3 g fat (1 g saturated), 4 mg cholesterol, 46 mg sodium, 7 mg potassium.

This version of the twice-baked Italian cookie is packed with extra flavor from colorful candied fruit.

Christmas Biscotti

½ **cup margarine** *or* **butter**
3 **cups all-purpose flour**
1 **cup sugar**
2 **eggs**
1 **egg yolk**
2½ **teaspoons baking powder**
1 **teaspoon aniseed, crushed,** *or* ¼
 teaspoon anise extract
1 **tablespoon finely shredded orange peel**
½ **cup chopped candied red cherries**
½ **cup chopped mixed candied fruit**
1 **egg white**
1 **teaspoon water**
1 **tablespoon sugar**

In a large mixing bowl beat the margarine or butter with an electric mixer on medium to high speed about 30 seconds or till softened. Add *1 cup* of the flour to the margarine. Then add the 1 cup sugar, whole eggs, egg yolk, baking powder, and aniseed or anise extract. Beat till thoroughly combined, scraping the sides of the bowl occasionally. Beat or stir in the remaining flour and orange peel. Stir in candied fruits. Divide dough in half.

Shape each portion into an 11x2x1-inch loaf. Place on an ungreased cookie sheet. Combine egg white and water. Brush mixture over loaves. Sprinkle with the 1 tablespoon sugar.

Bake in a 375° oven for 20 to 25 minutes or till lightly browned. Cool loaves on cookie sheet for 1 hour.

Cut each loaf diagonally into ½-inch-thick slices. Lay slices, cut side down, on the ungreased cookie sheet.

Bake in a 325° oven for 10 minutes. Turn slices over and bake for 10 to 15 minutes more or till dry and crisp. Remove cookies and cool on wire racks. Makes about 36.

Nutrition information per cookie: 100 calories, 2 g protein, 17 g carbohydrate, 3 g fat (1 g saturated), 18 mg cholesterol, 55 mg sodium, 18 mg potassium.

Christmas Eve Cookies

Whole Wheat-Brown Sugar Dough

1⅓ cups margarine *or* butter
2½ cups all-purpose flour
2 cups whole wheat flour
2 cups packed brown sugar
3 eggs
1 tablespoon baking powder
2 teaspoons vanilla
1½ teaspoons ground cinnamon
¾ teaspoon ground allspice
¼ teaspoon salt

🎁 In a large mixing bowl beat the margarine or butter with an electric mixer on medium to high speed about 30 seconds or till softened. Add *1 cup* of the all-purpose flour and *l cup* of the whole wheat flour to the butter. Then add the brown sugar, eggs, baking powder, vanilla, cinnamon, allspice, and salt. Beat till thoroughly combined. Beat in all of the remaining flour.

🎁 Divide dough into 3 portions. Use dough to make Date and Orange Pockets, Whole Wheat Spritz, and Sparkling Linzer Stars.

30

Date and Orange Pockets

With every bite, look forward to a luscious date, orange, and nut filling inside a tender cookie that is sweetened with a drizzle of browned butter frosting. Pictured on opposite page.

⅓ **of a recipe Whole Wheat-Brown Sugar Dough (see recipe, opposite)**
1 **8-ounce package chopped pitted dates**
⅓ **cup orange juice**
¼ **cup sugar**
¼ **cup chopped pecans *or* walnuts Golden Icing**

▮ Chill cookie dough about 1 hour or till firm enough to handle.
▮ Meanwhile, for filling, in a blender container or food processor bowl combine the dates, orange juice, sugar, and pecans or walnuts. Cover and blend or process till smooth, stopping to scrape the sides as needed.
▮ On a lightly floured surface, roll the dough to ⅛-inch thickness. Using a 2½-inch round cookie cutter, cut into rounds. Place rounds ½ inch apart onto ungreased cookie sheets. Spoon *1 level teaspoon* filling into center of *each* round. Fold *half* of the round over the filling, creating a half-moon shape. Seal cut edges of each round with the tines of a fork.

▮ Bake in a 375° oven for 7 to 9 minutes or till edges are firm and bottoms are lightly browned. Remove cookies and cool on wire racks.
▮ Spoon Golden Icing into a decorating bag fitted with a small round tip. Pipe Golden Icing onto each cooled cookie. (*Or*, with a spoon, drizzle Golden Icing atop cookies.) Makes about 40.

Golden Icing: In a small saucepan heat 2 tablespoons *butter* (not margarine) over medium-low heat for 10 to 12 minutes or till lightly browned. Remove from heat. Stir in ¾ cup sifted *powdered sugar*, ¼ teaspoon *vanilla*, and enough *milk* (about 4 teaspoons) to make icing of piping or drizzling consistency.

Nutrition information per cookie: 87 calories, 1 g protein, 15 g carbohydrate, 3 g fat (2 g saturated), 12 mg cholesterol, 41 mg sodium, 70 mg potassium.

31

Whole Wheat Spritz

Spritz cookies, a Christmas tradition, take on a terrific new flavor with Whole Wheat-Brown Sugar Dough. Pictured on page 30.

⅓ **of a recipe Whole Wheat-Brown Sugar Dough (see recipe, page 30)**
Colored sprinkles *and/or* colored sugars

🎁 *Do not chill dough. (Or,* if dough has been chilled, let stand at room temperature for 1 hour before using.)
🎁 Pack the dough into a cookie press. Force dough through press onto ungreased cookie sheets. Sprinkle cookies with colored sprinkles or sugars.
🎁 Bake in a 375° oven for 7 to 9 minutes or till edges are firm but not brown. Remove cookies and cool on wire racks. Makes about 40.

Nutrition information per cookie: 52 calories, 1 g protein, 8 g carbohydrate, 2 g fat (1 g saturated), 11 mg cholesterol, 35 mg sodium, 26 mg potassium.

Sparkling Linzer Stars

Show off your favorite homemade jam in these glitzy star-shaped cookies. Pictured on page 30.

⅓ **of a recipe Whole Wheat-Brown Sugar Dough (see recipe, page 30)**
Powdered sugar
¼ **cup seedless raspberry jam *or* cherry preserves**

🎁 Chill cookie dough about 1 hour or till firm enough to handle.
🎁 On a lightly floured surface, roll dough to ⅛-inch thickness. Using a 2- to 2½-inch star-shape cookie cutter, cut dough into star shapes. Place 1 inch apart onto ungreased cookie sheets. Then using a 1-inch star-shape cutter, cut out centers from *half* of the unbaked cookies. Remove centers and reroll dough to make more cookies.
🎁 Bake cookies in a 375° oven for 7 to 9 minutes or till edges are firm and bottoms are lightly browned. Remove cookies and cool on wire racks.
🎁 To assemble, sift powdered sugar over the tops of the cookies *with* holes in centers. Set aside. Spread about *½ teaspoon* of the jam or preserves onto the bottom of each cookie *without* a hole. Top each jellied cookie with a cookie with a hole, powdered sugar side up. Makes about 20.

Nutrition information per cookie: 114 calories, 1 g protein, 18 g carbohydrate, 4 g fat (3 g saturated), 22 mg cholesterol, 71 mg sodium, 56 mg potassium.

Gumdrop candies add a burst of color to the centers of these pure white cookies.

Meringue Snowflowers

  2 egg whites
½ **teaspoon vanilla**
¼ **teaspoon cream of tartar**
½ **cup sugar**
    Assorted gumdrops

▮ In a small mixing bowl let egg whites stand at room temperature for 30 minutes. Meanwhile, line a large cookie sheet with parchment paper. Set aside.

▮ Add the vanilla and cream of tartar to the egg whites. Beat with an electric mixer on medium speed till soft peaks form (tips curl). Gradually add sugar, *1 tablespoon* at a time, beating on high speed till stiff peaks form (tips stand straight) and sugar is *almost* dissolved.

▮ Spoon meringue mixture into a decorating bag fitted with a large star tip (½-inch opening). Pipe 1½-inch-diameter stars about 1½ inches apart onto prepared cookie sheet. Press a gumdrop into center of each star.

▮ Bake in a 300° oven about 15 minutes or till cookies just start to turn brown. Turn off oven. Let cookies dry in oven with the door closed for 10 minutes. Remove cookies and cool on wire racks. Makes about 48.

Nutrition information per cookie: 21 calories, 0 g protein, 5 g carbohydrate, 0 g fat (0 g saturated), 0 mg cholesterol, 4 mg sodium, 3 mg potassium.

*F*or multicolored ribbons, divide the dough into two or three portions. Tint each portion the color of your choice. Then pack the portions of dough into the press, side by side.

*H*oliday Ribbons

3½ cups all-purpose flour
1 teaspoon baking powder
1½ cups margarine *or* butter
1 cup sugar
1 egg
1 teaspoon vanilla
½ teaspoon lemon *or* orange extract *or* ¼ teaspoon almond *or* mint extract
Food coloring (optional)

In a medium bowl combine the flour and baking powder. Set aside.

In a large mixing bowl beat the margarine or butter with an electric mixer on medium speed about 30 seconds or till softened. Add the sugar and beat till fluffy. Add the egg, vanilla, and flavored extract. Beat well, scraping the sides of the bowl occasionally. Gradually add the flour mixture, beating till combined.

If desired, tint dough with food coloring. *Do not chill dough.*

Pack dough into a cookie press. Using the ribbon plate, force dough through the cookie press onto ungreased cookie sheets.

Bake in a 400° oven for 6 to 8 minutes or till edges are firm but not brown. Remove cookies and cool on wire racks. Makes about 60.

Nutrition information per cookie: 79 calories, 1 g protein, 8 g carbohydrate, 5 g fat (1 g saturated), 4 mg cholesterol, 60 mg sodium, 11 mg potassium.

*M*ocha Madeleines

2 eggs
1 teaspoon instant-coffee crystals
½ teaspoon vanilla
1 cup sifted powdered sugar
½ cup all-purpose flour
¼ cup unsweetened cocoa powder
⅛ teaspoon baking soda
½ cup margarine *or* butter, melted and cooled
Powdered sugar

▮ Grease and flour twenty-four 3-inch madeleine molds. Set aside.

▮ In a medium mixing bowl beat the eggs, coffee crystals, and vanilla with an electric mixer on high speed for 5 minutes. Gradually beat in 1 cup powdered sugar. Beat for 5 to 7 minutes more or till thick and satiny.

▮ Sift together the flour, cocoa powder, and baking soda. Sift *one-fourth* of the flour mixture over the egg mixture. Gently fold in. Fold in the remaining flour by fourths. Fold in melted margarine or butter. Spoon into prepared molds, filling ¾ full.

▮ Bake in a 375° oven for 10 to 12 minutes or till tops spring back when lightly touched. Cool in molds on a rack for 1 minute. Loosen cookies with a knife. Invert cookies onto wire racks, molded side up, and cool. Sift additional powdered sugar over tops. Store in the freezer. Makes 24.

Nutrition information per cookie: 71 calories, 1 g protein, 8 g carbohydrate, 4 g fat (1 g saturated), 18 mg cholesterol, 55 mg sodium, 58 mg potassium.

Choco-Mocha Madeleines: Prepare Mocha Madeleines as directed at left, *except* fold 1 ounce finely chopped *semisweet chocolate* into the batter along with the cooled margarine.

Nutrition information per cookie: 79 calories, 1 g protein, 8 g carbohydrate, 5 g fat (1 g saturated), 18 mg cholesterol, 54 mg sodium, 17 mg potassium.

A taste of honey adds a nice twist to the melt-in-the-mouth goodness of these traditional holiday cookies. So does rolling them in powdered sugar twice.

Honey Sand Balls

  1 **cup butter** (*not margarine*), **softened**
 ½ **cup sifted powdered sugar**
  2 **tablespoons honey**
  2 **cups all-purpose flour**
 ¾ **cup chopped walnuts**
  1 **teaspoon vanilla**
 ¼ **teaspoon salt**
     Sifted powdered sugar

In a large mixing bowl beat the butter, the ½ cup powdered sugar, and honey with an electric mixer on medium speed till combined. Beat or stir in the flour, walnuts, vanilla, and salt. Mix thoroughly, using your hands, if necessary.

Shape dough into 1-inch balls. Place balls 1½ inches apart onto greased cookie sheets.

Bake in a 325° oven for 14 to 16 minutes or till the cookies are very lightly browned. While cookies are still warm, roll them in powdered sugar. Cool cookies on wire racks. Roll cookies in powdered sugar again. Makes about 48.

Nutrition information per cookie: 74 calories,
1 g protein, 7 g carbohydrate, 5 g fat (3 g saturated),
10 mg cholesterol, 50 mg sodium, 16 mg potassium.

Brandy Snaps

½   **cup packed brown sugar**
⅓   **cup margarine *or* butter, melted**
¼   **cup molasses**
1   **tablespoon brandy**
¾   **cup all-purpose flour**
½   **teaspoon ground ginger**

▪ Line a cookie sheet with foil. Grease the foil. Set cookie sheet aside.

▪ In a medium mixing bowl stir together the brown sugar, margarine or butter, molasses, and brandy. Stir in the flour and ginger till thoroughly combined.

▪ Drop batter from a level teaspoon 5 inches apart on the prepared cookie sheet. (Bake only 4 or 5 at a time.)

▪ Bake in 350° oven for 5 to 6 minutes or till bubbly and deep golden brown.

▪ Cool cookies on cookie sheet for 1 to 2 minutes or till set. Quickly remove cookies, one at a time; with the flat side to the inside, roll each cookie around the greased handle of a wooden spoon. Cool. (If cookies harden before shaping, reheat about 1 minute or till softened.) Makes about 56.

Nutrition information per cookie: 27 calories, 0 g protein, 40 g carbohydrate, 1 g fat (0 g saturated), 0 mg cholesterol, 13 mg sodium, 22 mg potassium.

Sugared Stenciled Shapes

▪ Turn ordinary cookies into special holiday treats by using a stencil for the shape and shaking on powdered sugar or colored sugar. Look for small stencils in craft stores, or make your own.

To make stencils, cut a square of waxed paper to fit over cookies. In the center of the square draw a desired shape, tracing a design or using a tiny cookie or hors d'oeuvre cutter as a pattern. Using scissors, cut out the center shape.

To stencil cookies, place the stencil over the cookie. Sift desired sugar over the stencil. (Use powdered sugar or Chocolate Powdered Sugar for unfrosted baked cookies, and use colored sugar on unbaked or frosted baked cookies.) Then carefully remove the stencil.

Chocolate Powdered Sugar: Stir together 2 tablespoons *powdered sugar* and 1 teaspoon *unsweetened cocoa powder.*

*M*elting Moments

These cookies, each wrapped in crushed cornflakes and adorned with a cherry, are an English Christmas tradition.

1¼ cups all-purpose flour
1 teaspoon baking powder
¼ teaspoon baking soda
½ cup margarine *or* butter
⅓ cup sugar
1 egg yolk
½ teaspoon vanilla
1 slightly beaten egg white
½ cup cornflakes, crushed
14 candied cherries, halved

▮ In a medium mixing bowl stir together the flour, baking powder, and baking soda. Set aside.

▮ In a large mixing bowl beat the margarine or butter with an electric mixer on medium to high speed about 30 seconds or till softened. Add the sugar, egg yolk, and vanilla. Beat till thoroughly combined, scraping the sides of bowl occasionally. With the mixer on low speed, gradually add the flour mixture, beating till well mixed.

▮ Shape the dough into 1-inch balls. Roll in the egg white, then in the cornflakes. Place coated balls 2 inches apart onto ungreased cookie sheets. Top each ball with half of a candied cherry.

▮ Bake in 375° oven for 8 to 10 minutes or till set and slightly browned. Remove cookies and cool on wire racks. Makes about 28.

Nutrition information per cookie: 68 calories, 1 g protein, 8 g carbohydrate, 6 g fat (1 g saturated), 8 mg cholesterol, 63 mg sodium, 10 mg potassium.

Team these minty cookies with a flavored box of tea for a fun and festive gift.

Crisscross Mint Sandwich Creams

⅓ **cup margarine *or* butter**
¼ **cup shortening**
1⅓ **cups all-purpose flour**
½ **cup packed brown sugar**
¼ **cup sugar**
1 **egg**
1 **teaspoon vanilla**
½ **teaspoon baking powder**
½ **teaspoon baking soda**
   Sugar
2 **tablespoons softened margarine *or* butter**
2 **cups sifted powdered sugar**
½ **teaspoon mint flavoring *or* extract**
6 **drops red *or* green food coloring**
   Milk

🎁 In a large mixing bowl beat ⅓ cup margarine or butter and shortening with an electric mixer on medium to high speed about 30 seconds or till softened. Add about *half* the flour to the margarine mixture. Then add the brown sugar, sugar, egg, vanilla, baking

powder, and baking soda. Beat till thoroughly combined, scraping sides of bowl occasionally. Beat or stir in the remaining flour. If necessary, cover and chill dough till easy to handle.

🎁 Shape dough into ¾-inch balls. Place balls 2 inches apart onto ungreased cookie sheets. Using the tines of a fork dipped in additional sugar, flatten balls to about ¼-inch-thickness by pressing fork in 2 directions to form crisscross marks.

🎁 Bake in a 350° oven about 8 minutes or till bottoms are lightly browned. Remove cookies and cool on wire racks.

🎁 Meanwhile, for filling, in a small mixing bowl beat 2 tablespoons margarine or butter on medium speed for 30 seconds. Beat in 2 cups sifted powdered sugar, mint flavoring or extract, food coloring, and enough milk to make of spreading consistency. Spread filling on the flat side of *half* of the cooled cookies. Top with remaining cookies, flat sides down. Makes about 24.

Nutrition information per cookie: 138 calories, 1 g protein, 21 g carbohydrate, 6 g fat (1 g saturated), 9 mg cholesterol, 68 mg sodium, 28 mg potassium.

Dress these spiced cookies festively with a sprinkling of red and green sugar.

Sweet Anise Pretzels

3 cups all-purpose flour
1 teaspoon baking powder
½ teaspoon baking soda
1 to 1½ teaspoons finely crushed anise
   seed
½ teaspoon salt
½ cup margarine *or* butter
1 cup sugar
1 egg
1 teaspoon vanilla
⅔ cup buttermilk
   Colored sugar

In a medium mixing bowl stir together the flour, baking powder, baking soda, anise seed, and salt. Set aside.

In a large mixing bowl beat the margarine or butter with an electric mixer on medium to high speed about 30 seconds or till softened. Add the sugar and beat till fluffy. Add the egg and vanilla. Beat till thoroughly combined, scraping the sides of bowl occasionally. Alternately add the flour mixture and buttermilk to the margarine mixture, beating till well mixed. Cover and chill dough for 4 hours or overnight.

Divide dough in half. On a floured surface, roll *each* half into a 10x5-inch rectangle. Cut each half into twenty 5x½-inch strips. Roll each strip into a 9-inch rope. Form each rope into a pretzel shape by crossing one end over the other to form a circle, overlapping about 1½ inches from each end. Twist once at the point where dough overlaps. Lift ends across to the edge of the circle opposite them and press lightly to seal.

Place about 2 inches apart onto ungreased cookie sheets. Brush with water. Sprinkle with colored sugar.

Bake in a 425° oven for 5 to 6 minutes or till lightly browned. Remove cookies and cool on wire racks. Makes 40.

Nutrition information per cookie: 76 calories,
1 g protein, 12 g carbohydrate, 3 g fat (1 g saturated),
5 mg cholesterol, 77 mg sodium, 19 mg potassium.

Pistachios and a hint of spice are woven into a melt-in-your-mouth shortbread that's trimmed with a drizzle of chocolate.

Pistachio Sticks

1¼ **cups all-purpose flour**
 3 **tablespoons sugar**
¼ **teaspoon ground cardamom**
½ **cup butter** *(not margarine)*
¼ **cup finely chopped pistachio nuts**
½ **cup semisweet chocolate pieces**
 1 **teaspoon shortening**

🎁 In a medium mixing bowl stir together the flour, sugar, and cardamom. Using a pastry blender, cut in the butter till mixture resembles fine crumbs. Stir in the pistachio nuts. Form the mixture into a ball and knead till smooth.

🎁 On a lightly floured surface, pat or roll the dough into a 10x6-inch rectangle. Bake in a 325° oven for 25 to 30 minutes or just till the edges are lightly browned. While still warm, cut rectangle into 3x1-inch sticks. Remove cookies and cool on wire racks.

🎁 In a small heavy saucepan melt the chocolate pieces and shortening over low heat, stirring occasionally. Drizzle over cooled cookies. Makes 20.

Nutrition information per cookie: 105 calories, 1 g protein, 11 g carbohydrate, 7 g fat (3 g saturated), 12 mg cholesterol, 47 mg sodium, 38 mg potassium.

A spicy, pastrylike dough twists around sweet mincement filling.

Mincemeat Twists

2 cups all-purpose flour
⅓ cup packed brown sugar
½ teaspoon ground mace *or* ground
   nutmeg
¼ teaspoon baking powder
¾ cup margarine *or* butter
5 to 7 tablespoons cold water
⅔ cup prepared mincemeat
2 teaspoons finely shredded orange peel
   Milk
   Sugar

◈ In a large mixing bowl stir together the flour, brown sugar, mace or nutmeg, and baking powder. Using a pastry blender, cut in the margarine or butter till mixture resembles coarse crumbs. Sprinkle water, *1 tablespoon* at a time, over mixture till all is moistened, tossing gently with a fork. Form the mixture into a ball. Cover and chill about 30 minutes or till dough is easy to handle.

◈ In a small mixing bowl stir together the mincemeat and orange peel. Set aside. Divide dough into quarters. On a lightly floured surface, roll *two* of the quarters into 12x4-inch rectangles. Spread *each* rectangle with *half* of the mincemeat mixture. Roll the remaining quarters into 12x4-inch rectangles and carefully place over the mincemeat. Trim uneven edges. Cut each rectangle into twelve 4x1-inch strips. Twist each strip twice.

◈ Place twists about 2 inches apart onto ungreased cookie sheets. Bake in a 375° oven for 15 minutes. Remove from oven. Brush with milk and sprinkle with sugar. Return to oven and bake for 5 to 8 minutes more or till lightly browned. Remove twists and cool on wire racks. Makes 24.

Nutrition information per cookie: 116 calories, 1 g protein, 15 g carbohydrate, 6 g fat (1 g saturated), 0 mg cholesterol, 95 mg sodium, 40 mg potassium.

*L*ook for gold dragées in cooks' shops or mail-order catalogs that carry specialty cake and cookie decorating supplies.

*C*hocolate and Vanilla Wreaths

¾ **cup margarine *or* butter**
 2 **cups all-purpose flour**
¾ **cup sugar**
 1 **egg**
 1 **teaspoon vanilla**
½ **teaspoon ground cinnamon**
¼ **teaspoon baking powder**
 3 **tablespoons unsweetened cocoa powder**
 2 **tablespoons crème de cacao**
12 **candied red cherries, halved**
    Chocolate Decorating Frosting
    Gold dragées

👐 In a large mixing bowl beat the margarine or butter with an electric mixer on medium to high speed about 30 seconds or till softened. Add about *half* of the flour to the margarine. Then add the sugar, egg, vanilla, cinnamon, and baking powder. Beat till thoroughly combined, scraping sides of bowl occasionally. Beat or stir in remaining flour.
👐 Remove *half* of the dough from the bowl; cover and set aside. Stir the cocoa powder and crème de cacao into dough remaining in bowl. Cover. Chill both portions of dough about 30 minutes or till dough is easy to handle.
👐 On a lightly floured surface, shape *each* half of the dough into a 12-inch log. Cut each log into twenty-four ½-inch pieces. Roll each piece into a 6-inch rope. Place a light and a dark rope side by side and twist together 5 to 6 times. Shape twisted rope into a circle, gently pinching where ends meet. Place 2 inches apart onto ungreased cookie sheets. Place a cherry half over the pinched spot.
👐 Bake in a 375° oven for 8 to 10 minutes or till edges are firm and bottoms are lightly browned. Cool on cookie sheets for 1 minute. Remove cookies and cool on wire racks.

👐 Prepare Chocolate Decorating Frosting. Spoon into a decorating bag fitted with a small leaf tip. Make frosting leaves beside the cherries. Dot with gold dragées. Makes 24.

Chocolate Decorating Frosting: In a small mixing bowl beat 3 tablespoons *shortening* and ½ teaspoon *vanilla* with an electric mixer on medium speed for 30 seconds. Add ½ cup sifted *powdered sugar* and 3 tablespoons *unsweetened cocoa powder;* beat well. Add 2 teaspoons *milk.* Gradually beat in an additional ½ cup sifted *powdered sugar* and enough additional *milk* to make of piping consistency.

Nutrition information per cookie: 154 calories, 2 g protein, 20 g carbohydrate, 8 g fat (2 g saturated), 9 mg cholesterol, 74 mg sodium, 86 mg potassium.

Rich and buttery, these cookies are as joyfully anticipated as new toys under a Christmas tree.

Spicy Shortbread Nuggets

1¼ **cups all-purpose flour**
¼ **cup packed brown sugar**
½ **teaspoon aniseed, crushed**
¼ **teaspoon ground cinnamon**
⅛ **teaspoon ground cloves**
⅛ **teaspoon ground cardamom**
½ **cup margarine *or* butter**

In a large mixing bowl stir together the flour, brown sugar, aniseed, cinnamon, cloves, and cardamom. Using a pastry blender, cut in margarine till mixture resembles fine crumbs. Form mixture into a ball and knead till smooth.

Divide dough into 12 portions. On a lightly floured surface, roll *each* portion of dough into a 10-inch rope. Cut ropes into ½-inch pieces. Place pieces ½ inch apart onto ungreased shallow baking pans.

Bake in a 325° oven for 12 to 15 minutes or till the edges are firm and bottoms are lightly browned. Remove cookies and cool on paper towels. Makes about 240.

Nutrition information per cookie: 6 calories, 0 g protein, 1 g carbohydrate, 0 g fat (0 g saturated), 0 mg cholesterol, 5 mg sodium, 2 mg potassium.

Delicious little pastries filled with rich-flavored dried fruit.

Fruitcake Turnovers

2 **tablespoons sugar**
1 **teaspoon cornstarch**
½ **of a 6-ounce package (¾ cup) mixed dried fruit bits**
⅓ **cup apple *or* orange juice**
1 **teaspoon lemon juice**
¼ **teaspoon apple pie spice**
½ **teaspoon vanilla**
1 **11-ounce package piecrust mix**
   Colored sugar

▮ For filling, in a small saucepan stir together the sugar and cornstarch. Stir in the dried fruit, apple or orange juice, lemon juice, and apple pie spice. Cook and stir till thickened and bubbly. Cook and stir for 2 minutes more. Stir in vanilla. Remove from heat; cool.

▮ Prepare piecrust mix according to package directions for two-crust pie. Divide the dough in half. Form each half into a ball.

▮ On a lightly floured surface, roll *each* half to a 10½-inch square; trim to a 10-inch square. Cut into 2½-inch squares. Spoon ½ *teaspoon* of the filling onto *each* square. Moisten edges of each pastry square with water. Fold dough over filling to form triangles. With a fork, crimp edges to seal. Place the triangles onto greased cookie sheets. Lightly brush tops with water; sprinkle with colored sugar.

▮ Bake in a 375° oven about 15 minutes or till golden. Remove cookies and cool on wire racks. Makes 32.

Nutrition information per cookie: 74 calories, 1 g protein, 9 g carbohydrate, 4 g fat (1 g saturated), 0 mg cholesterol, 72 mg sodium, 34 mg potassium.

Frostings to Drizzle

▮ Accent your favorite drop, bar, sliced, shaped, or rolled cookies with a drizzle of simple stir-together icing. Just make sure the cookies are cool before you add the drizzle.

Chocolate Drizzle: Combine 1 cup sifted *powdered sugar* and 2 tablespoons *unsweetened cocoa* powder. Stir in 1 tablespoon *milk*. Stir in additional *milk*, 1 teaspoon at a time, till of drizzling consistency. Makes about ½ cup.

Coffee Drizzle: Dissolve ½ to 1 teaspoon instant *coffee crystals* in 1 tablespoon *water*. Stir in 1 cup sifted *powdered sugar*. Stir in additional *water*, 1 teaspoon at a time, till of drizzling consistency. Makes ½ cup.

Peanut Butter Drizzle: Combine 1 cup sifted *powdered sugar*, ¼ cup *peanut butter*, and 1 tablespoon *milk*. Stir in additional *milk* (2 to 3 tablespoons) till of drizzling consistency. Makes ⅔ cup.

Orange-Blossom Rosettes

For perfect frying results, use an oil that will not smoke at high temperatures, such as corn or peanut oil. Keep the oil at the right temperature. If it's too high, the rosette will burn before it cooks; too low and it will be greasy. To be sure of the temperature, use a deep-fat frying thermometer and be sure the tip doesn't touch the bottom of the pan.

> 1 **egg**
> 1 **tablespoon sugar**
> ½ **cup all-purpose flour**
> ¼ **cup milk**
> ½ **teaspoon grated orange peel**
> ¼ **cup orange juice**
> 1 **teaspoon vanilla**
> **Shortening** *or* **cooking oil for deep-fat frying**
> **Powdered sugar**

🎁 In a medium mixing bowl stir together the egg and sugar. Add the flour, milk, orange peel, orange juice, and vanilla. Beat with a rotary beater till smooth.

🎁 Heat a rosette iron in deep hot fat (375°) for 30 seconds. Remove iron from fat and drain on paper towels.

🎁 Dip the hot iron into the batter (batter should extend three-fourths of the way up the side of iron). Immediately dip iron in hot fat. Fry for 15 to 20 seconds or till golden. Lift iron out of fat, tipping slightly to drain.

🎁 Push rosette off the iron with a fork onto wire racks lined with paper towels. Repeat with remaining batter, reheating iron about 10 seconds each time.

🎁 To serve, sift powdered sugar over cooled cookies. Makes about 25.

Nutrition information per cookie: 38 calories, 1 g protein, 4 g carbohydrate, 2 g fat (1 g saturated), 9 mg cholesterol, 4 mg sodium, 13 mg potassium.

Crispy Snowflakes

Soft and pliable tortillas work best for making these lacy (and easy) snowflakes.

> 12 **8-** *or* **10-inch flour tortillas**
> **Shortening** *or* **cooking oil for deep-fat frying**
> **Powdered sugar**

🎁 Stack the tortillas and wrap in foil. Bake in a 350° oven for 10 minutes to soften.

🎁 Working with 2 tortillas at a time, use hors d'oeuvre or small cookie cutters to cut holes to resemble snowflakes.

🎁 In a large skillet fry one tortilla at a time in ½ inch hot fat (375°) for 30 to 60 seconds or till brown, turning once. Drain on wire racks lined with paper towels.

🎁 To serve, sift cookies with powdered sugar. Makes 12.

Nutrition information per cookie: 123 calories, 3 g protein, 19 g carbohydrate, 4 g fat (0 g saturated), 0 mg cholesterol, 0 mg sodium, 0 mg potassium.

Center the pizzelle iron's design on each cookie by dropping the pizzelle batter slightly off center toward the back of the iron's grid. As you lower the top, the batter will be pushed forward, distributing it evenly over the grid.

Coconut Pizzelles

1¾ **cups all-purpose flour**
1 **tablespoon baking powder**
3 **eggs**
¾ **cup sugar**
⅓ **cup margarine *or* butter, melted**
2 **teaspoons vanilla**
1½ **cups flaked coconut, toasted**
   Chocolate Glaze

In a small mixing bowl stir together the flour and baking powder. Set aside.

In a large mixing bowl beat eggs with an electric mixer on high speed about 4 minutes or till thick and lemon colored. With the mixer on medium speed, gradually beat in sugar. Beat in margarine or butter and vanilla. Add flour mixture and beat on low speed till combined.

Set aside ½ *cup* of the toasted coconut. Chop the remaining coconut (you should have ¾ cup). Fold the chopped coconut into the batter.

Heat an electric pizzelle iron according to manufacturer's directions. (Or, heat a nonelectric pizzelle iron on the range-top over medium heat till a drop of water sizzles on the grid. Reduce heat to medium-low.)

Place a slightly rounded tablespoon of batter slightly off center toward the back of grid. Close lid. Bake according to manufacturer's directions. (For a nonelectric iron, bake for 30 to 60 seconds or till golden, turning once.)

Turn wafer out onto a cutting board; cut into quarters. Transfer the quarters to a paper towel to cool completely. Repeat with the remaining batter.

Prepare Chocolate Glaze. Dip the rounded edge of each quarter into the glaze, then into the reserved coconut. Place on a rack till glaze is set. Makes 72 to 96.

Chocolate Glaze: Stir together 1 cup sifted *powdered sugar*, 2 tablespoons *unsweetened cocoa powder*, ¼ teaspoon *vanilla*, and enough *milk* (1 to 2 tablespoons) to make a mixture of glazing consistency.

Nutrition information per cookie: 43 calories, 1 g protein, 6 g carbohydrate, 2 g fat (1 g saturated), 9 mg cholesterol, 25 mg sodium, 19 mg potassium.

You can satisfy your craving for pie in just one or two bites with these tiny tarts.

Tiny Pumpkin Tarts

½ **cup margarine** *or* **butter, softened**
1 **3-ounce package cream cheese, softened**
1 **cup all-purpose flour**
  Pumpkin Filling

❦ For crust, in a medium mixing bowl beat the margarine or butter and cream cheese with an electric mixer on medium to high speed about 30 seconds or till combined. Stir in the flour. Cover and chill about 1 hour or till the dough is easy to handle.
❦ Form the chilled dough into a ball. Divide the dough into 24 equal portions. Roll each portion into a ball. Place each ball into an ungreased 1¾-inch muffin cup. Press the dough evenly against the bottom and up the sides of cup. Cover and set aside.
❦ Prepare Pumpkin Filling. Fill *each* pastry-lined muffin cup with a rounded *teaspoon* Pumpkin Filling.
❦ Bake in a 325° oven about 30 minutes or till pastry is golden and filling is puffed. Cool slightly in pans. Remove tarts from pans and cool on wire racks. Makes 24.

Pumpkin Filling: In a small mixing bowl stir together 1 *egg*, ½ cup canned *pumpkin*, ¼ cup *sugar*, ¼ cup *milk*, and 1 teaspoon *pumpkin pie spice*.

Nutrition information per tart: 66 calories, 1 g protein, 6 g carbohydrate, 4 g fat (1 g saturated), 13 mg cholesterol, 44 mg sodium, 28 mg potassium.

Tiny Lemon-Coconut Tarts: Prepare Tiny Pumpkin Tarts as directed at left, *except* omit the Pumpkin Filling. For lemon-coconut filling, divide ¼ cup *coconut* among the pastry-lined muffin cups. In a small mixing bowl combine 2 *eggs*, ½ cup *sugar*, 2 tablespoons melted *margarine or butter*, ½ teaspoon finely shredded *lemon peel*, and 1 tablespoon *lemon juice*. Spoon mixture over coconut in pastry-lined muffin cups. Bake as directed.

Nutrition information per tart: 86 calories, 1 g protein, 8 g carbohydrate, 5 g fat (2 g saturated), 22 mg cholesterol, 57 mg sodium, 20 mg potassium.

Tiny Spiced Fruit Tarts: Prepare Tiny Pumpkin Tarts as directed at left, *except* omit the Pumpkin Filling. For spiced fruit filling, in a small saucepan combine 1½ cups chopped *mixed dried fruit* and 1½ cups *apple juice or water*. Bring to boiling; reduce heat. Cover and simmer about 8 minutes or till fruit is very tender. Drain. Stir in ¼ cup *orange marmalade*, 1 teaspoon ground *nutmeg*, and ¼ teaspoon ground *cloves*. Spoon mixture into pastry-lined muffin cups. Bake as directed.

Nutrition information per tart: 78 calories, 1 g protein, 10 g carbohydrate, 4 g fat (1 g saturated), 4 mg cholesterol, 42 mg sodium, 61 mg potassium.

How easy! All you have to do is add a three-ingredient filling to frozen puff pastry, cut, twist, and bake.

Pictured on the cover.

Almond Twists

½ of a 17½-ounce package (1 sheet)
  frozen puff pastry
½ cup almond paste
1 egg
¼ cup packed brown sugar
1 cup sifted powdered sugar
¼ teaspoon vanilla
  Milk
  Coarsely chopped sliced almonds
  (optional)

🎁 Let pastry stand at room temperature for 20 minutes or till easy to roll. On a lightly floured surface, unfold pastry. Roll into a 14-inch square. Using a fluted pastry wheel, cut square in half.

🎁 For filling, in a small mixing bowl crumble the almond paste. Add the egg and brown sugar. Beat with an electric mixer on medium speed till well mixed.

🎁 Spread filling over *one portion* of pastry. Place remaining pastry half on top of filling. Using the fluted pastry wheel, cut dough into seven 14x1-inch strips. Then cut *each* strip crosswise into *quarters.* (You should have 28 pieces.) Twist each piece twice.

🎁 Place twists about 2 inches apart onto ungreased cookie sheets. Bake in a 400° oven for 12 to 15 minutes or till golden. Remove twists and cool on wire racks.

🎁 Meanwhile, for icing, in a small mixing bowl stir together the powdered sugar, vanilla, and enough milk (1 to 2 tablespoons) to make of drizzling consistency. Drizzle icing over twists. If desired, sprinkle with almonds. Makes 28.

Nutrition information per cookie: 80 calories,
1 g protein, 10 g carbohydrate, 4 g fat (0 g saturated),
8 mg cholesterol, 36 mg sodium, 36 mg potassium.

A tangy mixture of cranberries, orange marmalade, and walnuts peeks through the top of each cutout star cookie.

Cranberry Stars

2 cups cranberries
½ cup orange marmalade
2 tablespoons honey
¼ cup finely chopped walnuts
4½ cups all-purpose flour
1 teaspoon baking soda
¼ teaspoon salt
1 cup shortening
½ cup margarine *or* butter
2 cups sugar
2 eggs
¼ cup milk
1 teaspoon vanilla
 Milk *or* water
 Sugar

ii In a medium saucepan cook the cranberries, marmalade, and honey, covered, till mixture boils and berries pop. Uncover; cook 5 to 10 minutes more or till the consistency of thick jam. Stir in the walnuts. Cool mixture to room temperature.

ii In a medium mixing bowl stir together the flour, baking soda, and salt. Set aside.

ii In a large mixing bowl beat the shortening and margarine or butter with an electric mixer on medium to high speed about 30 seconds or till softened. Add the sugar; beat till fluffy. Add the eggs, milk, and vanilla; beat well. Gradually add the flour mixture to the egg mixture; mix well. Divide dough into quarters. Cover and chill about 3 hours or till dough is easy to handle.

ii On a lightly floured surface, roll *1 portion* of the dough to ⅛-inch thickness. Cut cookies with a 2-inch round cookie cutter. Using a small star cutter, cut a star from the center of *half* of the cookies. Place a scant *1 teaspoon* cranberry mixture on *each* plain round. Top with cutout cookie; seal edges with fork. Brush with milk or water; sprinkle with sugar. Place onto ungreased cookie sheets.

ii Bake in a 375° oven for 8 to 10 minutes or till lightly browned. Cool cookies on wire racks. Repeat with remaining dough. Makes about 60.

Nutrition information per cookie: 119 calories, 1 g protein, 17 g carbohydrate, 6 g fat (1 g saturated), 7 mg cholesterol, 44 mg sodium, 22 mg potassium.

Cherry-Cheese Pinwheels

⅓ **cup shortening**
⅓ **cup margarine *or* butter**
2 **cups all-purpose flour**
¾ **cup sugar**
1 **egg**
1 **tablespoon milk**
1½ **teaspoons baking powder**
1 **teaspoon vanilla**
¼ **teaspoon salt**
1 **3-ounce package cream cheese,
    softened**
¼ **cup sugar**
¼ **teaspoon almond extract**
½ **cup chopped maraschino cherries**
¼ **cup finely chopped toasted almonds**

🎁 In a mixing bowl beat the shortening and margarine or butter with an electric mixer on medium to high speed about 30 seconds or till softened. Add about *half* of the flour to the shortening mixture. Then add the ¾ cup sugar, egg, milk, baking powder, vanilla, and salt. Beat till thoroughly combined, scraping sides of bowl occasionally. Then beat or stir in the remaining flour. Divide dough in half. Cover and chill about 3 hours or till dough is easy to handle.

🎁 Meanwhile, in a small mixing bowl stir together the softened cream cheese, ¼ cup sugar, and almond extract. Stir in the chopped cherries.

🎁 On a lightly floured surface, roll *each* half of the dough into a 10-inch square. With a pastry wheel or sharp knife, cut each square into sixteen 2½-inch squares. Place ½ inch apart onto ungreased cookie sheets. Use a knife to cut 1-inch slits from each corner to center. Drop a level teaspoon of the cream cheese mixture in each center. Fold every other tip to center to form a pinwheel. Sprinkle chopped nuts in center and press firmly to seal.

🎁 Bake in a 350° oven for 8 to 10 minutes or till edges are firm and cookies are slightly puffed. Cool on cookie sheets for 1 minute. Remove cookies and cool on wire racks. Makes about 32.

Nutrition information per cookie: 106 calories, 1 g protein, 13 g carbohydrate, 6 g fat (2 g saturated), 10 mg cholesterol, 65 mg sodium, 28 mg potassium.

Brighten your holiday cookie sampler with these plump mincemeat-filled cookies.

Christmas Tree Treats

2 cups all-purpose flour
1 cup whole wheat flour
1 tablespoon baking powder
1 teaspoon ground cinnamon
½ teaspoon ground nutmeg
¼ teaspoon salt
½ cup margarine *or* butter
3 eggs
½ cup milk
2 tablespoons honey
1 slightly beaten egg white
2 tablespoons honey
1 cup All-Fruit Mincemeat, drained (see recipe, page 13), *or* prepared mincemeat
½ cup broken walnuts
   Colored sugar (optional)

In a large mixing bowl stir together the all-purpose flour, whole wheat flour, baking powder, cinnamon, nutmeg, and salt. Cut in the margarine or butter till pieces are the size of small peas. Stir together the eggs, milk, and 2 tablespoons honey. Add to the flour mixture; stir till combined. Divide dough in half.

On a lightly floured surface, roll out *half* of the dough to ⅛-inch thickness. Using a 4-inch tree cookie cutter, cut 18 pastry trees, rerolling dough as necessary. Place onto lightly greased cookie sheets.

In a small mixing bowl stir together the egg white and remaining 2 tablespoons honey. Brush trees with mixture. In another bowl stir together the All-Fruit Mincemeat or prepared mincemeat and walnuts. Place 1 rounded tablespoon filling in the center of each tree.

Roll and cut remaining dough as directed above. Place the remaining trees over the trees with filling. Seal the edges with the tines of a fork. Brush the egg white mixture over each cookie. If desired, sprinkle with colored sugar.

Bake in a 375° oven for 10 to 12 minutes or till lightly browned. Remove cookies and cool on wire racks. Makes 18.

Nutrition information per cookie: 202 calories, 4 g protein, 28 g carbohydrate, 9 g fat (2 g saturated), 36 mg cholesterol, 209 mg sodium, 117 mg potassium.

Honey, molasses, and a collection of spices flavor this traditional German Christmas cookie.

Lebkuchen

1 egg
¾ cup packed brown sugar
½ cup honey
½ cup dark molasses
3 cups all-purpose flour
1 teaspoon ground cinnamon
½ teaspoon baking soda
½ teaspoon ground cloves
½ teaspoon ground ginger
¼ teaspoon ground cardamom
½ cup chopped almonds
½ cup finely chopped mixed candied fruit
   and peels
   Lemon Glaze
   Additional chopped mixed candied
   fruit and peels

In a small mixing bowl beat the egg with an electric mixer on high speed about 1 minute. Add the brown sugar; beat on medium speed till light and fluffy. Add the honey and molasses. Beat well.

In a large mixing bowl stir together the flour, cinnamon, baking soda, cloves, ginger, and cardamom. Add egg mixture. Stir by hand till combined. (Dough will be stiff.) Stir in the almonds and ½ cup candied fruit and peels. Cover and chill dough about 3 hours or till dough is easy to handle.

Divide dough in half. On a lightly floured surface, roll *each* half to a 12x8-inch rectangle. Cut into 2-inch squares. Place onto lightly greased cookie sheets.

Bake in a 350° oven for 8 to 10 minutes or till edges are lightly browned. Remove from oven. Cool on cookie sheets for 1 minute. Remove cookies and cool on wire racks.

Brush cookies with Lemon Glaze while they are still warm. Garnish with additional candied fruit and peels. Allow glaze to dry well.

Store, tightly covered, overnight or up to 7 days to soften. Makes 48.

Lemon Glaze: In a small mixing bowl stir together 1½ cups sifted *powdered sugar,* 1 tablespoon melted *margarine or butter,* 1 tablespoon *lemon juice,* and enough *water* (3 to 4 teaspoons) to make glaze of drizzling consistency.

Nutrition information per cookie: 93 calories, 1 g protein, 20 g carbohydrate, 1 g fat (0 g saturated fat), 4 mg cholesterol, 15 mg sodium, 64 mg potassium.

Paint holiday pictures on each cutout cookie with a tiny paintbrush and a dab of food coloring.

Painted Sour Cream Sugar Cookies

½   **cup margarine *or* butter**
2½ **cups all-purpose flour**
1   **cup sugar**
½   **cup dairy sour cream**
1   **egg**
1   **teaspoon baking powder**
1   **teaspoon vanilla**
¼   **teaspoon baking soda**
    Dash salt
1   **teaspoon finely shredded lemon peel**
2   **cups sifted powdered sugar**
½   **teaspoon vanilla**
    Milk
    Food coloring

■ In a large mixing bowl beat the margarine or butter with an electric mixer on medium to high speed about 30 seconds or till softened. Add about *half* of the flour to the margarine. Then add the sugar, sour cream, egg, baking powder, 1 teaspoon vanilla, baking soda, and salt. Beat till thoroughly combined, scraping sides of bowl occasionally. Beat or stir in the remaining flour and lemon peel. Divide dough in half. Cover and chill for 1 to 2 hours or till dough is easy to handle.

■ On a well floured surface, roll *each* half of the dough to ⅛- to ¼-inch thickness. Using cookie cutters, cut into desired shapes. With a spatula, transfer cookies to ungreased cookie sheets, placing them ½ inch apart.

■ Bake in a 375° oven for 7 to 8 minutes or till edges are firm and bottoms are very lightly browned. Remove and cool on wire racks.

■ For glaze, in a medium mixing bowl stir together the powdered sugar, ½ teaspoon vanilla, and enough milk (2 to 3 tablespoons) to make mixture of glazing consistency. Spread the top of each cooled cookie with some of the glaze. Allow glaze to dry completely. Using a small paintbrush, paint designs on each cookie with food coloring. Makes about 48.

Nutrition information per cookie: 77 calories, 1 g protein, 13 g carbohydrate, 3 g fat (1 g saturated), 6 mg cholesterol, 38 mg sodium, 13 mg potassium.

Pumpkin Cookies

4½ **cups all-purpose flour**
2 **teaspoons baking powder**
1 **teaspoon baking soda**
1½ **teaspoons ground cinnamon**
½ **teaspoon salt**
½ **teaspoon ground ginger**
½ **teaspoon ground nutmeg**
1¼ **cups shortening**
1 **cup sugar**
1 **cup packed brown sugar**
2 **eggs**
1 **teaspoon finely shredded orange peel**
1 **teaspoon vanilla**
1 **16-ounce can pumpkin**
   Powdered sugar

In a mixing bowl stir together the flour, baking powder, baking soda, cinnamon, salt, ginger, and nutmeg. Set aside.

In a large mixing bowl beat the shortening with an electric mixer on medium to high speed for 30 seconds. Add the sugar and brown sugar; beat till fluffy. Add the eggs, orange peel, and vanilla; beat well. Add *half* of the flour mixture to the shortening mixture; beat well. Add the pumpkin. Add the remaining flour mixture, beating till well mixed. Divide dough in half. Cover and chill about 3 hours or till dough is easy to handle. (Dough will still be very soft.)

On a well floured surface, roll *each* half of the dough to ¼-inch thickness. Cut with a 2-inch cutter. Place 2½ inches apart onto ungreased cookie sheets.

Bake in a 375° oven about 10 minutes or till edges are lightly browned. Remove cookies and cool on wire racks. Dust cookies with powdered sugar. (If desired, use a doily as a stencil.) Makes about 70.

Nutrition information per cookie: 89 calories, 1 g protein, 13 g carbohydrate, 4 g fat (1 g saturated), 6 mg cholesterol, 39 mg sodium, 34 mg potassium.

A molasses-and-spice-flavored dough, perfect for making plump little gingerbread people.

Pictured on the cover and on page 4.

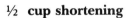

Gingerbread Cutouts

½ **cup shortening**
2½ **cups all-purpose flour**
½ **cup sugar**
½ **cup molasses**
1 **egg**
1 **tablespoon vinegar**
1 **teaspoon baking powder**
1 **teaspoon ground ginger**
½ **teaspoon baking soda**
½ **teaspoon ground cinnamon**
½ **teaspoon ground cloves**
  Powdered Sugar Icing (optional)
  Decorative candies (optional)

In a mixing bowl beat the shortening with an electric mixer on medium to high speed for 30 seconds. Add about *half* of the flour. Then add the sugar, molasses, egg, vinegar, baking powder, ginger, baking soda, cinnamon, and cloves. Beat till combined, scraping bowl occasionally. Beat or stir in remaining flour.

Cover and chill about 3 hours or till the dough is easy to handle.

Divide chilled dough in half. On a lightly floured surface, roll *each* half of the dough to ⅛-inch thickness. Using 2½-inch cookie cutters, cut dough into desired shapes. Place 1 inch apart onto greased cookie sheets.

Bake in a 375° oven for 5 to 6 minutes or till edges are lightly browned. Cool on cookie sheets for 1 minute. Remove cookies and cool on wire racks. If desired, prepare Powdered Sugar Icing. Decorate cookies with icing and, if desired, decorative candies. Makes about 36.

Powdered Sugar Icing: In a small mixing bowl stir together 1 cup sifted *powdered sugar,* ¼ teaspoon *vanilla,* and enough *milk* (1 to 2 tablespoons) to make an icing of drizzling consistency.

Nutrition information per cookie: 78 calories, 1 g protein, 12 g carbohydrate, 3 g fat (1 g saturated), 6 mg cholesterol, 22 mg sodium, 53 mg potassium.

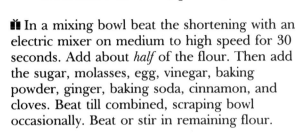

Chocolate Cutouts

3 cups all-purpose flour
½ cup unsweetened cocoa powder
1 teaspoon baking soda
¾ teaspoon ground ginger
½ teaspoon baking powder
½ teaspoon ground cinnamon
¼ teaspoon salt
¼ teaspoon ground cloves
⅔ cup shortening
½ cup sugar
1 egg
½ cup dark corn syrup
¼ cup milk
1 egg white
1 tablespoon water
Decorating Icing

▮ In a mixing bowl stir together the flour, cocoa powder, baking soda, ginger, baking powder, cinnamon, salt, and cloves. Set aside.
▮ In a large mixing bowl beat the shortening with an electric mixer on medium to high speed for 30 seconds. Add the sugar and beat till fluffy. Add the whole egg, corn syrup, and milk; beat well. Beat in the flour mixture, stirring in the last part with a spoon till well mixed. Divide dough in half. Cover and chill about 1 hour or till dough is easy to handle.
▮ On a lightly floured surface, roll *each* half of dough to ⅛-inch thickness. Cut with desired cookie cutters. Place onto greased cookie sheets. In a small mixing bowl stir together the egg white and water. Brush mixture on cutouts.
▮ Bake in a 375° oven for 5 to 7 minutes or till slightly puffed and set. Cool on cookie sheets for 1 minute. Remove cookies and cool on wire racks. Pipe on Decorating Icing with decorating bag and writing tip. Makes about 48.

Decorating Icing: In a medium mixing bowl stir together 3 cups sifted *powdered sugar* and enough *milk* (3 to 5 tablespoons) to make icing of piping consistency.

Nutrition information per cookie: 98 calories, 1 g protein, 17 g carbohydrate, 3 g fat (1 g saturated), 5 mg cholesterol, 38 mg sodium, 60 mg potassium.

Anise adds a licoricelike taste to these holiday-favorite sugar cookies.

*A*nise Cutouts

    4 cups all-purpose flour
    1 tablespoon baking powder
    ½ teaspoon salt
    ¾ cup margarine *or* butter
    ⅔ cup shortening
1½ cups sugar
    2 eggs
    2 tablespoons milk
    2 teaspoons vanilla
    8 to 12 drops anise oil

❖ In a mixing bowl stir together the flour, baking powder, and salt. Set aside.

❖ In a large mixing bowl beat the margarine or butter and shortening with an electric mixer on medium to high speed about 30 seconds or till softened. Add the sugar and beat till fluffy. Add the eggs, milk, vanilla, and anise oil; beat well. Add the flour mixture and beat till well mixed. Divide dough in half.

❖ Cover and chill about 3 hours or till the dough is easy to handle.

❖ On a lightly floured surface, roll *each* half to ⅛-inch thickness. Cut with desired cookie cutters. Place onto ungreased cookie sheets.

❖ Bake in a 375° oven for 7 to 8 minutes or till edges are firm and bottoms are lightly browned. Remove cookies and cool on wire racks. Frost and decorate as desired. Makes about 72.

Nutrition information per cookie: 78 calories, 1 g protein, 9 g carbohydrate, 4 g fat (1 g saturated), 6 mg cholesterol, 55 mg sodium, 20 mg potassium.

Cookies Kids Can Help Make

Keep holiday traditions. Bring out the paper chains, strings of lights, and Christmas storybooks. Then gather children in the kitchen to bake cookies in jolly shapes—precious angels, chubby Santas, and snowy mountains. You'll see . . . laughter is the best-kept tradition of all.

Simple Snowflakes
(see recipe, page 71)

Roly-Poly Santas
(see recipe, page 66)

Beneath the mountain's snow, a delectable morsel of mint or chocolate awaits.

Snow-Topped Chocolate Mountains

⅓ cup margarine *or* butter
⅔ cup sifted powdered sugar
2 squares (2 ounces) semisweet chocolate, melted and cooled
1 teaspoon vanilla
1¼ cups all-purpose flour
2 tablespoons milk
24 pastel cream mint kisses *or* milk chocolate kisses
   Fluffy Frosting

🎁 In a mixing bowl beat margarine or butter with an electric mixer on medium to high speed about 30 seconds or till softened. Gradually beat in the powdered sugar. Beat in melted chocolate and vanilla. Beat or stir in the flour and milk.

🎁 Shape a well-rounded teaspoon of dough around each kiss. Place cookies pointed side up onto greased cookie sheets.

🎁 Bake in a 350° oven for 10 to 12 minutes or till bottoms are lightly browned. Remove cookies and cool on wire racks.

🎁 Frost peaks of cookies with Fluffy Frosting. Makes 24.

Fluffy Frosting: In a small mixing bowl beat 2 tablespoons *shortening* and ½ teaspoon *vanilla* for 30 seconds. Gradually add ½ cup sifted *powdered sugar*, mixing well. Add 1 tablespoon *milk*. Beat in enough additional sifted *powdered sugar* (about ¾ cup) to make a frosting of fluffy consistency.

Nutrition information per cookie: 122 calories, 1 g protein, 17 g carbohydrate, 6 g fat (2 g saturated), 0 mg cholesterol, 36 mg sodium, 37 mg potassium.

Youngsters can enjoy creating these simple-to-make angels using pretzels for wings and mint-wafer candies for heads.

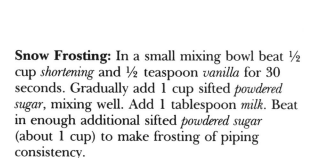

Christmas Angels

½ cup margarine *or* butter
⅓ cup sugar
2 teaspoons finely shredded orange *or* lemon peel
1 teaspoon orange *or* lemon juice
1⅓ cups all-purpose flour
¼ teaspoon baking soda
40 small pretzels
Snow Frosting
Pastel mint wafers (yellow, pink, and white) *or* halved large gumdrops

🎁 In a large mixing bowl beat margarine or butter with an electric mixer on medium to high speed about 30 seconds or till softened. Add sugar and beat till fluffy. Beat in the orange or lemon peel and juice. With mixer on low speed, gradually add flour and soda, beating till mixture resembles coarse crumbs. Using your hands, knead till dough is smooth.
🎁 On an ungreased cookie sheet shape *1 tablespoon* dough into a triangle about 2½ inches long and 2 inches wide. For wings, lightly press a pretzel into the triangle at each side near the tip of the triangle. Repeat with the remaining dough and pretzels.
🎁 Bake in a 325° oven for 10 to 15 minutes or till edges are firm and bottoms are very lightly browned. With a pancake turner, lift cookies to wire racks to cool.
🎁 Prepare the Snow Frosting. For the heads, use frosting to attach the pastel mint wafers or gumdrops to the top of the triangle. Decorate angels as desired with frosting. Makes 20.

Snow Frosting: In a small mixing bowl beat ½ cup *shortening* and ½ teaspoon *vanilla* for 30 seconds. Gradually add 1 cup sifted *powdered sugar*, mixing well. Add 1 tablespoon *milk*. Beat in enough additional sifted *powdered sugar* (about 1 cup) to make frosting of piping consistency.

Nutrition information per cookie: 250 calories, 3 g protein, 34 g carbohydrate, 12 g fat (3 g saturated), 0 mg cholesterol, 327 mg sodium, 48 mg potassium.

Stir up these confection cookies in a jiffy—they require no baking. To be sure each cherry (representing Rudolph's bright red nose) stays attached, press it securely onto the antlers.

Rudolph's Antlers

  1 **6-ounce package (1 cup) semisweet chocolate pieces**
 ½ **of a 6-ounce package (½ cup) butterscotch pieces**
  1 **3-ounce can chow mein noodles**
 12 **maraschino cherries, halved**

▮ In a medium saucepan melt the chocolate and butterscotch pieces over low heat, stirring occasionally. Remove the pan from the heat. Stir in the chow mein noodles.

▮ Spoon about 1 tablespoon of the mixture onto a waxed-paper-lined cookie sheet. Use 2 teaspoons to shape the mixture into a V-shape cookie about 2 inches wide to resemble antlers. Press a cherry half in the center. Repeat for remaining cookies.

▮ Chill the cookies on the cookie sheet in the refrigerator for 1 to 2 hours or till the cookies are firm. Then store the cookies in the refrigerator in a covered container for up to 5 days. Makes 24.

Nutrition information per cookie: 72 calories, 1 g protein, 10 g carbohydrate, 4 g fat (1 g saturated), 0 mg cholesterol, 19 mg sodium, 37 mg potassium.

Tiny Christmas Trees

  1 **cup margarine *or* butter**
 ⅔ **cup sugar**
 ¼ **teaspoon almond extract**
2⅓ **cups all-purpose flour**
  2 **drops yellow food coloring**
 ¼ **teaspoon green food coloring**
     Colored coarse decorating sugar

▮ In a large mixing bowl beat the margarine or butter with an electric mixer on medium to high speed about 30 seconds or till softened. Add the sugar and beat till fluffy. Beat in the almond extract. Add the flour and beat till well mixed.

▮ Remove about 2 tablespoons of the dough and knead in the yellow food coloring. Knead the green food coloring into remaining dough.

▮ Roll dough into ¼-inch-diameter ropes and cut ropes into ¼-inch pieces. Round each piece slightly.

▮ Place green balls in a pyramid shape in rows of five, four, three, and two balls on an ungreased cookie sheet. Place a small ball of yellow dough on top for the star. Add a small piece of green dough to the bottom for a trunk. Repeat with remaining dough. Sprinkle with colored sugar.

▮ Bake in a 325° oven for 12 to 15 minutes or till edges are firm and bottoms are lightly browned. Makes about 60.

Nutrition information per cookie: 47 calories, 0 g protein, 4 g carbohydrate, 3 g fat (1 g saturated), 0 mg cholesterol, 36 mg sodium, 6 mg potassium.

Little balls of dough bake together to create this traditional holiday symbol.

Sweet little treats hide inside these powdered sugar-coated cookies. Take a bite and see.

Surprise Snowballs

¾ **cup margarine *or* butter**
½ **cup sugar**
¼ **teaspoon salt**
 1 **egg**
½ **teaspoon vanilla**
1¾ **cups all-purpose flour**
   Candy-and-milk-chocolate-covered peanuts, gumdrops, jelly beans, *and/or* candy-coated milk chocolate pieces
¾ **cup sifted powdered sugar**

🎁 In a large mixing bowl beat margarine or butter with an electric mixer on medium to high speed about 30 seconds or till softened. Add the sugar and salt and beat till fluffy. Add egg and vanilla. Beat till thoroughly combined, scraping the sides of bowl occasionally. With mixer on low speed, gradually add the flour, beating till well combined.

🎁 Shape the dough into 1-inch balls. Press a piece of desired candy in center of each and shape the dough around it so you can't see the candy. Place balls about 2 inches apart onto ungreased cookie sheets.

🎁 Bake in a 350° oven about 15 minutes or till edges are lightly browned. Place powdered sugar in a plastic bag. While cookies are still warm, transfer 2 or 3 cookies at a time to the bag of powdered sugar. Gently shake cookies in powdered sugar till coated. Cool on wire racks. When cool, gentle shake cookies again in powdered sugar. Makes about 36.

Nutrition information per cookie: 85 calories, 1 g protein, 10 g carbohydrate, 5 g fat (1 g saturated), 6 mg cholesterol, 63 mg sodium, 18 mg potassium.

Skating Bears and Sledding Teddies

Ginger Cookies were never so fun!

1 cup margarine *or* butter
⅔ cup packed brown sugar
⅔ cup corn syrup *or* molasses
4 cups all-purpose flour
2 teaspoons ground cinnamon
1 teaspoon ground ginger
¾ teaspoon baking soda
¾ teaspoon ground cloves
1 beaten egg
1½ teaspoons vanilla
Miniature semisweet chocolate pieces
Decorating Frosting (optional)
Medium candy canes (about 6 inches) **(optional)**
Graham crackers (optional)

In a medium saucepan heat and stir margarine or butter, brown sugar, and corn syrup or molasses over medium heat till margarine melts and sugar dissolves. Pour into a large mixing bowl; cool 5 minutes.

Meanwhile, in a mixing bowl combine flour, cinnamon, ginger, soda, and cloves. Stir egg and vanilla into margarine mixture. Stir in flour mixture. Cover and chill about 2 hours or till dough is easy to handle.

To make each adult bear, shape some of the dough into one 1½-inch ball (for body), one 1-inch ball (for head), three ¼-inch balls (for nose and ears), two 1¾-inch-long by ½-inch-wide logs (for arms), and two 1½-inch-long by ¾-inch-wide logs (for legs). If desired, taper legs so slightly wider at hand and feet ends.

❧ On an ungreased cookie sheet flatten the 1½-inch ball for body to a 2-inch round. Attach the 1-inch ball for head; flatten to a 1½-inch round. Attach the ¼-inch balls to the head for nose and ears. Attach the 1¾-inch-long logs for arms and the 1½-inch-long logs for legs. (*Do not* attach legs for sledding teddies.)

❧ To make youth bears, make balls and logs a little smaller than those for the adult bears. To make baby bears, make balls and logs a little smaller than those for the youth bears. Assemble as for adult bear, flattening the body and head. Attach nose, ears, arms, and legs. (*Do not* attach legs for sledding teddies.) For bears holding hands, assemble side by side on cookie sheet. Press hands together.

❧ To decorate all bears before baking, press in chocolate pieces, point side up, for eyes. For paws, press chocolate pieces, point side down, into ends of arms and legs. (Press into arms only if making skating bears.) Bake in a 325° oven 15 minutes for adults, 12 minutes for youths, or 8 minutes for babies or till edges are lightly browned. Transfer to wire racks; cool.

❧ For skating bears, cut small rectangles of heavy foil; diagonally trim ends to resemble skate blades. Attach under end of bears' legs with Decorating Frosting, leaving the longer side of each foil "blade" showing.

❧ For sledding teddies, make a sled by attaching 2 candy canes (for runners) to a whole graham cracker with the frosting. Attach bodies upright to the sled with the frosting. (If necessary, cut the rounded end of the body off to make it easier to attach to the sled.) Then use the frosting to attach legs to body and sled as if bear were sitting with legs out front on the sled. To have a baby bear sitting atop the larger bear, attach the baby bear's body to the larger bear with the frosting. Attach the legs with frosting to the larger bear's legs. Makes 12 adult or 21 youth or 36 baby bear cookies.

Decorating Frosting: In a mixing bowl beat ¼ cup *shortening* and ¼ teaspoon *vanilla* with an electric mixer on medium to high speed for 30 seconds. Gradually beat in 1¼ cups sifted *powdered sugar*. Beat in enough *milk* (about 1 tablespoon) to make a frosting of spreading consistency.

Nutrition information per adult cookie: 385 calories, 5 g protein, 55 g carbohydrate, 16 g fat (3 g saturated), 18 mg cholesterol, 253 mg sodium, 102 mg potassium.

Chubby cookie replicas of jolly old Saint Nick are sure to please kids of all ages.

Pictured on the cover and on page 59.

Roly-Poly Santas

1 **cup margarine *or* butter**
½ **cup sugar**
1 **tablespoon milk**
1 **teaspoon vanilla**
2¼ **cups all-purpose flour**
    Red paste food coloring
    Miniature semisweet chocolate pieces
    Snow Frosting

In a large mixing bowl beat margarine or butter with an electric mixer on medium to high speed about 30 seconds or till softened. Add sugar and beat till fluffy. Beat in milk and vanilla. Add flour and beat till well combined. Remove *1 cup* of dough. Stir red paste food coloring into remaining dough till desired color is attained.

Shape each Santa by making one ¾-inch ball and four ¼-inch balls from white dough. From red dough, shape one 1-inch ball and five ½-inch balls. On an ungreased cookie sheet flatten the 1-inch red ball for body to ½-inch thickness. Attach white ¾-inch ball for head; flatten to ½ inch. Attach four ½-inch red balls for arms and legs. Shape remaining ½-inch red ball into a hat. Place white ¼-inch balls at ends of arms and legs for hands and feet. Use chocolate pieces for eyes and buttons.

Bake in a 325° oven 12 to 15 minutes or till edges are lightly browned. Cool 2 minutes on cookie sheets. Remove and cool on wire racks.

Prepare Snow Frosting. With a decorating bag fitted with a plain tip, pipe a mustache, a band of icing on hat, cuffs at hands and feet, down the front, and at the bottom of jacket. Use a star tip to pipe beard and pom-pom on hat. Makes 12.

Snow Frosting: In a large mixing bowl beat ½ cup *shortening* and ½ teaspoon *vanilla* for 30 seconds. Gradually add 1⅓ cups sifted *powdered sugar*, mixing well. Add 1 tablespoon *milk*. Gradually beat in 1 cup additional sifted *powdered sugar* and enough *milk* (3 to 4 teaspoons) to make frosting of piping consistency.

Nutrition information per cookie: 409 calories, 3 g protein, 46 g carbohydrate, 25 g fat (5 g saturated), 0 mg cholesterol, 181 mg sodium, 45 mg potassium.

A classic combination, cherries and chocolate come together in these colorful, buttery cookies.

Chocolate-Dipped Cherry Shortbread

½ **cup maraschino cherries, chopped**
1¼ **cups all-purpose flour**
3 **tablespoons sugar**
½ **cup butter** *(not margarine)*
1 **tablespoon milk**
2 *or* 3 **drops red food coloring (optional)**
½ **cup semisweet chocolate pieces**
2 **teaspoons shortening**
3 **ounces vanilla-flavored candy coating, chopped**
2 **teaspoons shortening**

🎁 Drain cherries on paper towels.

🎁 In a medium mixing bowl stir together the flour and sugar. Using a pastry blender, cut in the butter till mixture resembles fine crumbs. Stir in the cherries, milk, and, if desired, food coloring. Form into a ball; knead till smooth.

🎁 Shape dough into 1-inch balls. Place 2 inches apart onto ungreased cookie sheets. Using the bottom of a glass, slightly flatten balls to ½-inch thickness.

🎁 Bake in a 325° oven about 20 minutes or till edges are firm and bottoms are lightly browned. Remove and cool on wire racks.

🎁 Melt together the chocolate pieces and 2 teaspoons shortening. Dip *half* of the cookies into melted chocolate mixture. Place on a wire rack till chocolate is firm.

🎁 Melt together candy coating and 2 teaspoons shortening. Dip the remaining cookies into mixture. Place on a wire rack till coating is firm. Makes about 24.

Nutrition information per cookie: 109 calories, 1 g protein, 12 g carbohydrate, 7 g fat (3 g saturated), 10 mg cholesterol, 43 mg sodium, 38 mg potassium.

Kids will enjoy shaping these fanciful sugar-cookie snails.

Sugar Snails

¾ **cup margarine** *or* **butter**
¾ **cup sugar**
1 **egg**
1 **teaspoon vanilla**
2 **cups all-purpose flour**
¼ **teaspoon baking powder**
  Whole cloves
  Milk
  Colored sugar

In a large mixing bowl beat margarine or butter with an electric mixer on medium to high speed about 30 seconds or till softened. Add sugar and beat till fluffy. Add egg and vanilla and beat well.

In a medium mixing bowl stir together the flour and baking powder. Gradually add the flour mixture to the margarine mixture, beating well. Divide dough in half. Cover and chill about 30 minutes or till dough is easy to handle.

On a lightly floured surface, roll about *2 tablespoons* of the dough into a 10-inch rope. On an ungreased cookie sheet, coil the rope into a circle. Bend back the end of the rope to make the head. Add two whole cloves for antennae. Repeat with remaining dough. Brush the snails with milk and sprinkle them with colored sugar.

Bake in a 375° oven for 10 to 12 minutes or till lightly browned. Remove cookies and cool on wire racks. Makes about 24.

Nutrition information per cookie: 116 calories, 1 g protein, 15 g carbohydrate, 6 g fat (1 g saturated), 9 mg cholesterol, 73 mg sodium, 18 mg potassium.

Peanut-Butter-and-Jelly Posies

Save some of these jelly-filled thumbprint cookies for Santa, if you can.

1½ **cups all-purpose flour**
½ **teaspoon baking powder**
½ **teaspoon baking soda**
¼ **teaspoon salt**
½ **cup margarine** *or* **butter**
½ **cup peanut butter**
⅓ **cup sugar**
⅓ **cup packed brown sugar**
3 **tablespoons orange juice**
Red *and/or* **green jelly**

 In a medium mixing bowl stir together the flour, baking powder, soda, and salt. Set aside.

 In a large mixing bowl beat margarine or butter and peanut butter with an electric mixer on medium to high speed about 30 seconds or till softened. Add sugar and brown sugar and beat till fluffy. Add orange juice and beat well. With mixer on low speed, gradually add flour mixture to peanut butter mixture, beating till well mixed.

 Shape the dough into 1-inch balls. Place about 1 inch apart onto ungreased cookie sheets. Press down the center of each ball with your thumb.

 Bake in a 350° oven for 8 to 10 minutes or till lightly browned. Cool on cookie sheets for 2 minutes. Remove cookies and cool on wire racks.

 Spoon about ¼ *teaspoon* jelly into the center of *each* cookie. Makes about 36.

Nutrition information per cookie: 82 calories, 1 g protein, 10 g carbohydrate, 4 g fat (1 g saturated), 0 mg cholesterol, 78 mg sodium, 43 mg potassium.

69

*T*he frosted-cookie stacks begin to soften after about 5 days. For longer storage, store the cookies unfrosted at room temperature or freeze them. Then frost and assemble the cookies at serving time.

*S*taggered Stars

2½ **cups all-purpose flour**
 1 **teaspoon ground ginger**
 ¾ **teaspoon baking soda**
 ½ **teaspoon ground cinnamon**
 ¼ **teaspoon salt**
 ¼ **teaspoon ground cloves**
 ½ **cup shortening**
 ½ **cup sugar**
 1 **egg yolk**
 ½ **cup molasses**
 1 **tablespoon vinegar**
    Vanilla Icing
    Colored sugar (optional)

■ In a medium mixing bowl stir together the flour, ginger, baking soda, cinnamon, salt, and cloves. Set aside.

■ In a large mixing bowl beat shortening with an electric mixer on medium to high speed for 30 seconds. Add sugar and beat till fluffy. Add egg yolk, molasses, and vinegar and beat well. Stir in flour mixture. Divide dough in half.

■ On a lightly floured surface, roll *each* half of the dough to ⅛-inch thickness. Cut with 2-inch and/or 3-inch star-shape cutters. Place onto greased cookie sheets.

■ Bake in a 375° oven for 5 to 6 minutes or till edges just begin to brown (watch closely, cookies brown quickly). Cool on cookie sheets for 1 minute. Remove cookies and cool on wire racks.

■ Frost tops of stars with Vanilla Icing, leaving points exposed. Staggering points, stack pairs of cookies together. If desired, sprinkle top cookie with colored sugar. Makes 36 to 48.

Vanilla Icing: In a mixing bowl stir together 3 cups sifted *powdered sugar*, 1 teaspoon *vanilla*, and enough *milk* (2 to 3 tablespoons) to make icing of spreading consistency. If desired, divide and tint with food coloring.

Nutrition information per cookie: 110 calories, 1 g protein, 20 g carbohydrate, 3 g fat (1 g saturated), 6 mg cholesterol, 34 mg sodium, 52 mg potassium.

Simple Snowflakes

Poke snowflakelike designs into these delicate cutout cookies with drinking straws. Then shower them with a sprinkling of powdered sugar.

Pictured on the cover and on page 59.

2	**cups all-purpose flour**
1½	**teaspoons baking powder**
½	**teaspoon ground cinnamon**
¼	**teaspoon salt**
¼	**teaspoon ground nutmeg**
½	**cup margarine *or* butter**
¼	**cup shortening**
¾	**cup sugar**
1	**egg**
1	**tablespoon orange juice *or* lemon juice**
	Powdered sugar

In a medium mixing bowl stir together the flour, baking powder, cinnamon, salt, and nutmeg. Set aside.

In a large mixing bowl beat margarine or butter and shortening with an electric mixer on medium to high speed about 30 seconds or till softened. Add sugar and beat till fluffy. Add egg and orange or lemon juice and beat well. Add flour mixture and beat or stir till well mixed. Divide dough in half. Cover and chill at least 3 hours or till dough is easy to handle.

On a lightly floured surface, roll *each* half to ⅛-inch thickness. Cut with a 2½-inch scalloped round or star-shape cookie cutter. Using two sizes of drinking straws, cut random holes from the cutout dough, twisting straws slightly, if necessary. Place cutouts onto ungreased cookie sheets.

Bake in a 375° oven for 7 to 8 minutes or till edges are lightly browned. Remove cookies and cool on wire racks. Sift powdered sugar generously over cool cookies. Makes about 36.

Nutrition information per cookie: 79 calories, 1 g protein, 10 g carbohydrate, 4 g fat (1 g saturated), 6 mg cholesterol, 59 mg sodium, 11 mg potassium.

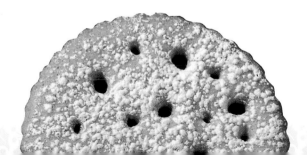